Transcribed SCORES

the jimi hendrix experience
axis: bold as love

EXPERIENCE HENDRIX
"A JIMI HENDRIX FAMILY COMPANY"

Exclusively Distributed By

HAL•LEONARD CORPORATION
7777 W. BLUEMOUND RD. P.O. BOX 13819 MILWAUKEE, WI 53213

ISBN 0-7935-6062-4

For all works contained herein:
Unauthorized copying, arranging, adapting, recording or public performance is an infringement of copyright.
Infringers are liable under the law.

Visit Hal Leonard Online at
www.halleonard.com

Visit EXPERIENCE HENDRIX Online at
www.jimi-hendrix.com

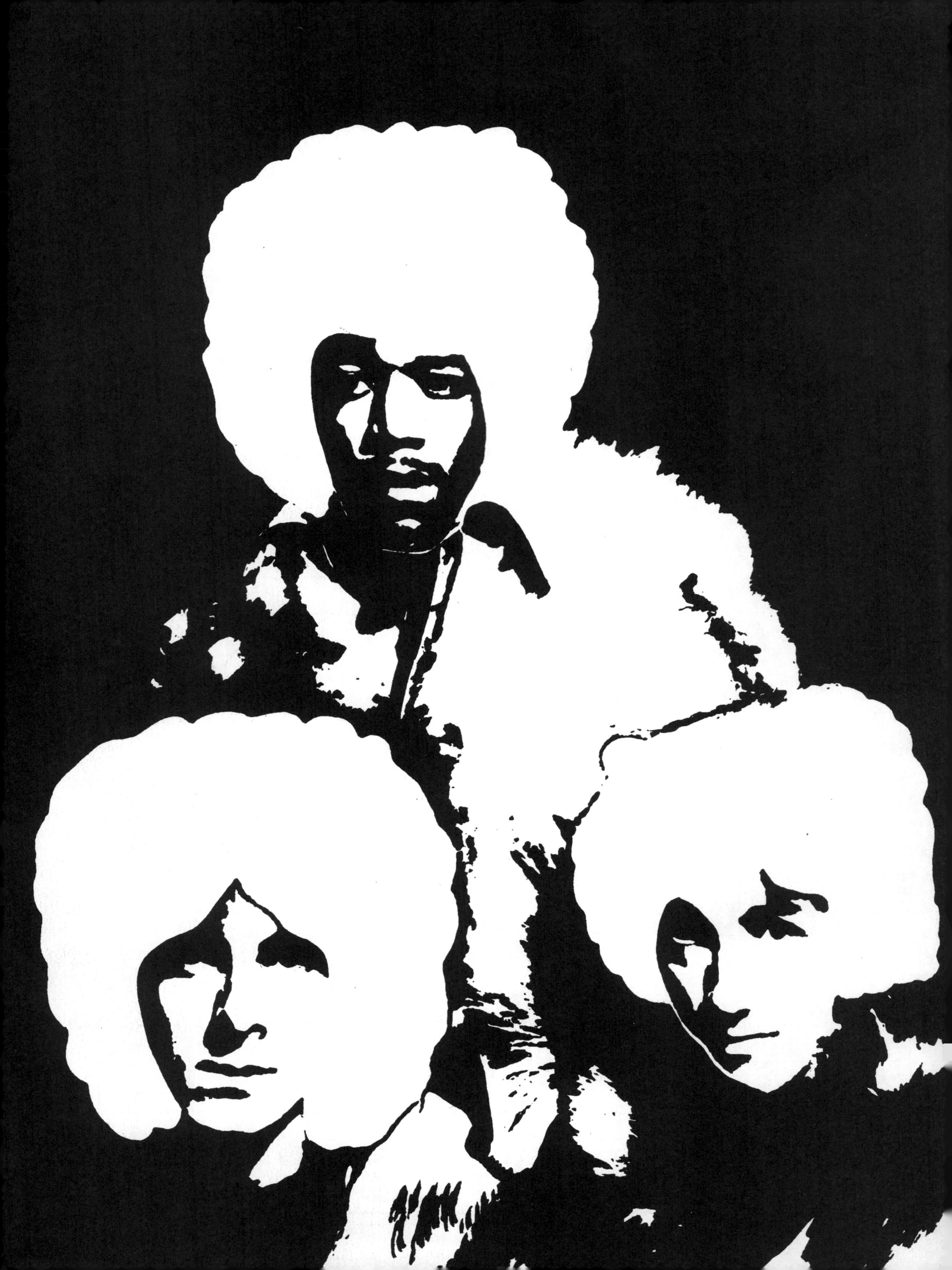

Page	Title
4	INTRODUCTION
54	AIN'T NO TELLING
166	BOLD AS LOVE
114	CASTLES MADE OF SAND
6	EXP
73	IF 6 WAS 9
156	LITTLE MISS LOVER
63	LITTLE WING
140	ONE RAINY WISH
128	SHE'S SO FINE
22	SPANISH CASTLE MAGIC
8	UP FROM THE SKIES
36	WAIT UNTIL TOMORROW
99	YOU GOT ME FLOATIN'
189	GUITAR NOTATION LEGEND
190	BASS NOTATION LEGEND

All selections written by Jimi Hendrix, except "She's So Fine" by Noel Redding
All lyrics, except "She's So Fine" © 1968 renewed 1996 Experience Hendrix, L.L.C. (ASCAP).
Used by permission. All rights reserved.
"She's So Fine" © 1968 Joint Music Co., Inc. (BMI). Used by permission. All rights reserved.

A VOYAGE TO THE COSMOS

Jimi Hendrix recorded the thirteen stellar tracks of *Axis: Bold As Love* in 1967, in the wake of his tremendous reception at Monterey and the huge impact that *Are You Experienced?* and the outrageousness of his music had begun to make on the youth of the world. The generation that embraced Jimi was going through its changes, experimenting with new lifestyles and rebellion, and developing its own culture of flamboyant dress and extravagant gesture. They were ready for Jimi, and he was willing to take them out, showing them the brave new worlds that one could see by the light of the stars, if only one would dare to fly.

Jimi's energetic stage manner and much-vaunted pyrotechnics inspired headlines and newspaper copy wherever they went. By the Summer of Love, Jimi, Mitch and Noel had been touring the States as their music broke on the American airwaves. They played the Fillmore in San Francisco to the tumultuous acclaim of that town's hippies and freaks, and they returned to England in August to put the finishing touches on Axis and to gird themselves for the months of heavy touring that would set the stage for its release, which occurred in November, 1967. The band played material from the new album as they toured Europe through the end of that year, and continued their primal assault on America in 1968.

If *Experienced?* can be seen as a thunderbolt that released shock waves through the minds of those in its path, *Axis* is a comet on its way to outer space with Jimi sitting right on top of it, saying, "Hop on board!" The spacey sound of the album, as captured by producer Chas Chandler and the brilliant engineer Eddie Kramer, is deeper, more spiritual, and musically self-indulgent than that of its predecessor. Nowhere is this more evident than on the title track, "Bold As Love" which ends the album on the English version, but for some inexplicable reason is sandwiched in the middle of side two on the American release. Unlike *Experienced?* there are no track substitutions, only a slight difference of track order between this and the British release. After Jimi states his ballad theme, accented by droning, bluesy riffs on the middle strings, Mitch's tom-toms lead into a coda of absolutely magnificent, lyrical guitar work that is phased and processed as it flies around the universe. The same kind of processing is carried to the nth degree on the album's opener, "EXP," after the intro rap to the "spaceman" Paul Corusoe. Hendrix' guitar - and parts of "Paul Revere's Ride," feedback, radio noise, and a mess of other sounds get melanged through Eddie Kramer's audio meat-grinder as they go careening from speaker to speaker and - again - out to outer space.

The mystical nature of the album is heightened by Jimi's intimate vocal textures, the studio mikes catching his philosophical asides and metaphysical ramblings, as on the anthemic "If 6 Was 9," as he muses about the uniqueness of his own iconoclastic lifestyle: "Dig – 'cause I got my own world to live through and I ain't gonna copy you." Then, the inimitable oratorio of ..."white-collared conservative flashin' down the street, pointing their plastic finger at me...I'm gonna wave my freak flag high!...Go on, Mr. Businessman, you can't dress like me...I got my own life to live. I'm the one who's got to die when it's time for me to die. So let me live my life the way I want to." And once that epitome of bohemianism and cosmic far-outness is uttered, Hendrix goes off into the outer limits again with his guitar and his wah-wah pedal and a million other sonic gadgets.

Throughout the album, Hendrix swings on the axis of the universe, feeling his sonic oats and spouting wisdom and beautiful melodies like he was breathing them - which he was. The man had so many musical ideas coursing through him all the time that he couldn't wait to write them down, scribbling on pieces of paper or improvising with his guitar. And so, *Axis: Bold As Love* stands today as a record of that magical obsession, and we who study it here in tranquillity may benefit from its bounty. Though much of it has to do with studio trickery and experimentation, all of it is built on the solid musicianship and the artistic vision of the man who invented it, and the deftness of the two frizzy-haired cohorts who drove the engine with bass and drums and rode along with him on those flights of fancy, keeping up with him as only the most intimate of partners could.

We've tried to keep this in mind as we laid out this volume, with its exact and exacting transcriptions of bass, drum and guitar parts. There is much to be learned by modern musicians from these written-out footprints of posterity. You will notice in studying these charts that the dance was highly choreographed. Not only did these guys click on a cosmic level, but all their moves depended on precision timing and orchestration - and a profound musical vision.

-Noë "the G" Goldwasser
Founding Editor, *Guitar World*

Exp

Words and Music by Jimi Hendrix

Beautiful "noise," elaborate soundscapes and unusual coloristic effects on the guitar are all a part of Hendrix's musical legacy, but in some instances they still remain a bit of an enigma, a tough nut to crack for transcribers sifting through the sands of time.

Harmonic and microphonic feedback are the main components of this piece, but only the former could be accurately, albeit subjectively, notated. This type of feedback is directly related to the harmonic overtone series and may be initiated in several ways. One surefire method is to lightly touch a vibrating open string at the proper position or node while in close proximity to the amp. For example, if the fifth string were ringing out an open A and you wanted feedback an octave above that, you'd just make brief contact with the sting directly over the twelfth fret. If done at the seventh fret instead, the result will be E, an octave and a fifth above open A; at the fifth, an even higher A; at the fourth, C#, and so on.

Fundamental tone (same as the actual pitch) feedback is readily achieved by placing the headstock of your guitar against the speaker cabinet. Experiment with the vibrato bar, combine the two aforementioned techniques, and make some of your own close encounters of the "Third Stone" kind.

Announcer:	Good evening ladies and gentlemen.
	Welcome to radio station EXP.
	Tonight we are featuring an interview with a very peculiar looking gentleman
	who goes by the name of Mr. Paul Corusoe, on the dodgy subject of: Are there
	or are there not flying saucers or...ahem, UFO's?
	Um...Please, Mr. Corusoe, could you give us your regarded opinion on this
	nonsense about spaceships, and even space people?
Mr. Corusoe:	Thank you.
	As you all know, you just can't believe everything you see and hear. Can you?
	Now, if you'll excuse me, I must be on my way.
Announcer:	Bu...but, but...glub...I, I don't believe it.

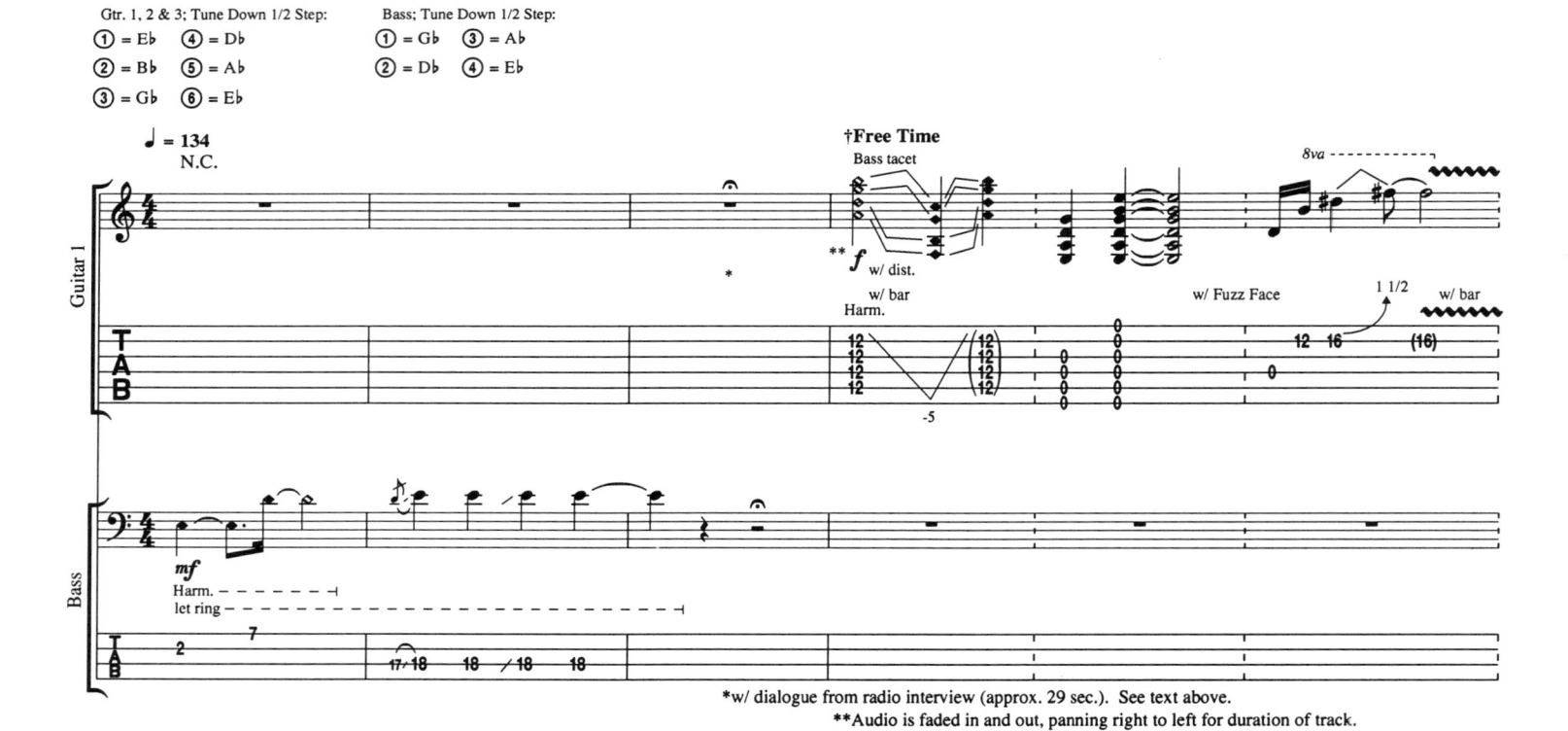

Gtr. 1, 2 & 3; Tune Down 1/2 Step:
① = Eb ④ = Db
② = Bb ⑤ = Ab
③ = Gb ⑥ = Eb

Bass; Tune Down 1/2 Step:
① = Gb ③ = Ab
② = Db ④ = Eb

*w/ dialogue from radio interview (approx. 29 sec.). See text above.
**Audio is faded in and out, panning right to left for duration of track.
† No time signature.

Copyright © 1968, 1977 by EXPERIENCE HENDRIX, L.L.C.
Copyright Renewed 1996
All Rights Controlled and Administered by EXPERIENCE HENDRIX, L.L.C.
All Rights Reserved

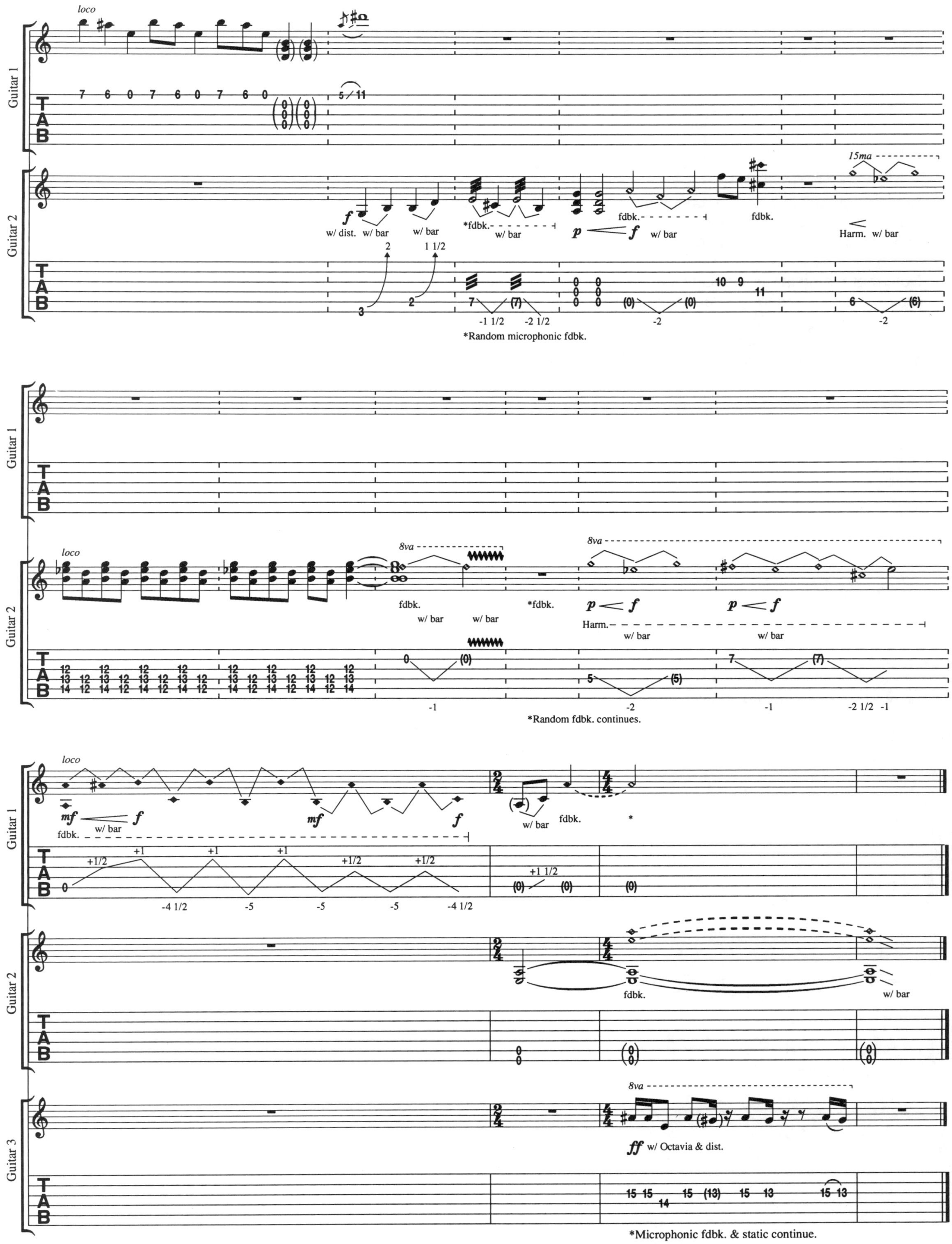
Guitar 1
Guitar 2
Guitar 3
loco
w/ dist.
w/ bar
*fdbk.
fdbk.
Harm.
15ma
8va
*Random microphonic fdbk.
*Random fdbk. continues.
w/ Octavia & dist.
*Microphonic fdbk. & static continue.

Up From The Skies

Words and Music by Jimi Hendrix

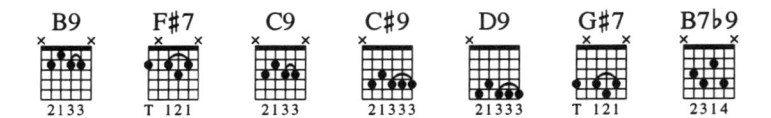

Chords: B9, F#7, C9, C#9, D9, G#7, B7♭9

"EXP" segues into this song concerning a visiting extra-terrestrial and its queries regarding life on this planet, providing some subtle tongue-in-cheek social commentary in the process. Meanwhile, a "jazzy" groove is laid down by a trio of Earth denizens: Mitch (with brushes in hand), Jimi (with wah-wah pedal at foot) and Noel.

Note that the guitar accompaniment throughout the verses has been reduced to a chord-chart type of format. For greater ease of reading, you'll need to refer to the chord diagrams in order to achieve the correct voicings. Incidentally, if these forms, with their numerical designations, are "alien" to you and you're curious as to their origin, then check out your library for textbooks dealing with basic harmony. Some additional information may also be found in the player's notes for "If 6 Was 9."

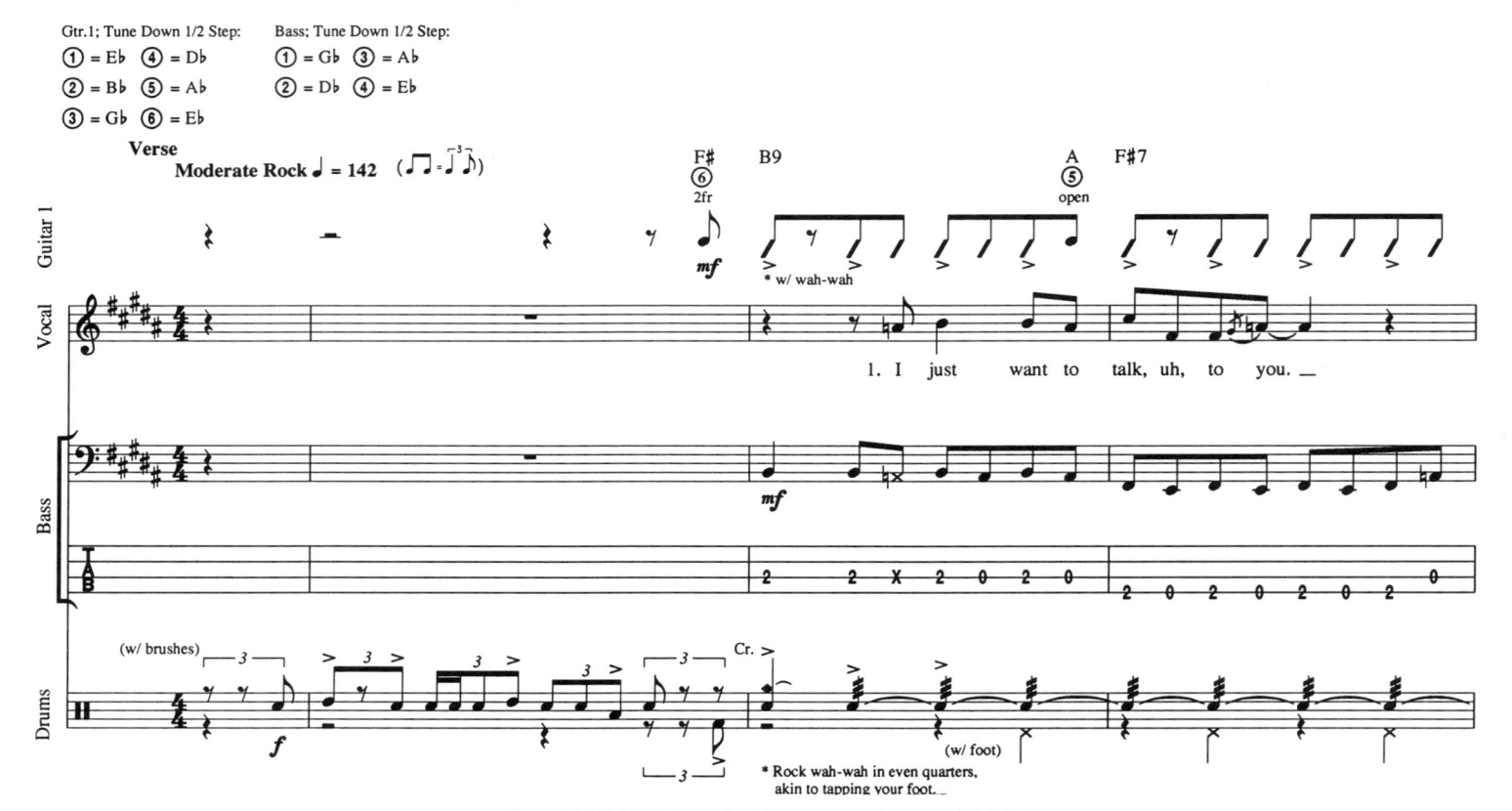

Gtr.1; Tune Down 1/2 Step:
① = E♭ ④ = D♭
② = B♭ ⑤ = A♭
③ = G♭ ⑥ = E♭

Bass; Tune Down 1/2 Step:
① = G♭ ③ = A♭
② = D♭ ④ = E♭

Verse
Moderate Rock ♩ = 142

1. I just want to talk, uh, to you.

* Rock wah-wah in even quarters, akin to tapping your foot.

Copyright © 1968, 1977 by EXPERIENCE HENDRIX, L.L.C.
Copyright Renewed 1996
All Rights Controlled and Administered by EXPERIENCE HENDRIX, L.L.C.
All Rights Reserved

Lyrics:

I won't, uh, do you no harm. I just want to know about your dif'rent lives on this here people farm. I heard some of you got your fam'lies living in cages tall and cold. And some just stay there and dust away,

Guitar 1
Vocal
Bass
Drums
B9 C9 F#7 B9 C9
past the age of old. Is this
F#7 B9 C9 C F#7
3fr
true? Please let me talk to you.
Verse
C#9 D9 G#7 C#9 D9
2. I just want to know a - bout the rooms be - hind your minds.

11

things like "Love the world," and uh, a "Let your fan-cy flow."

Is this true? Please let me talk to you. Let me talk to

(cont. in notation)

* Gtr. 1 panning left to right every two measures throughout Bridge.

Bridge lyrics:
you. I have lived here be-fore the days of ice. And of course this is why I'm so con-cerned.

14

Vocal
Guitar 1
Bass
Drums
C9
B9
world _ that's burned. ___
let ring
C#7
N.C.(C#7)
(B)
A smell of the world that has burned. ___
Spoken: Yeah, _ well,
1/2

(C♯)
(B)
Vocal
may-be, umm...
may - be it's just a... _
change of
Guitar 1
let ring
1/4
full full full full full
full
Bass
Drums
(C♯)
(B)
Vocal
cli-mate.
Mmm, _ hmm.
Well,
Guitar 1
let ring
Bass
Drums

Lyrics:

I can dig it. I can dig it, ba-by. I just want to see.

Verse

3. So where do I pur-chase my tick-et? I'd just like to have a ring-side seat. I want to know a-bout the new Moth-er Earth, I want to hear and see ev-'ry-thing. I

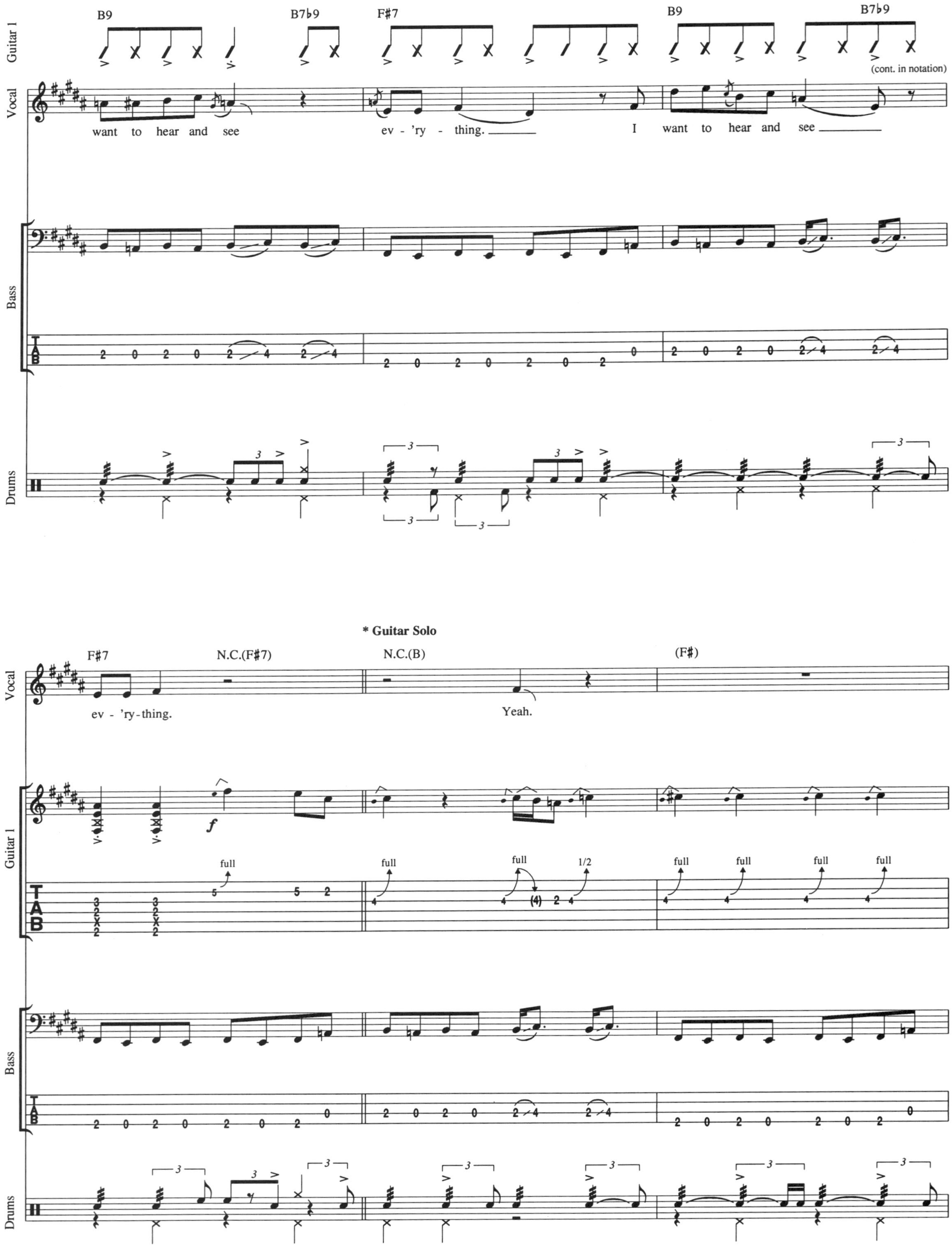

* Gtr. 1 panning right to left till end of song.

Vocal
Guitar 1
Bass
Drums
(B)
(F♯)
(B)
full
full
full
full
even

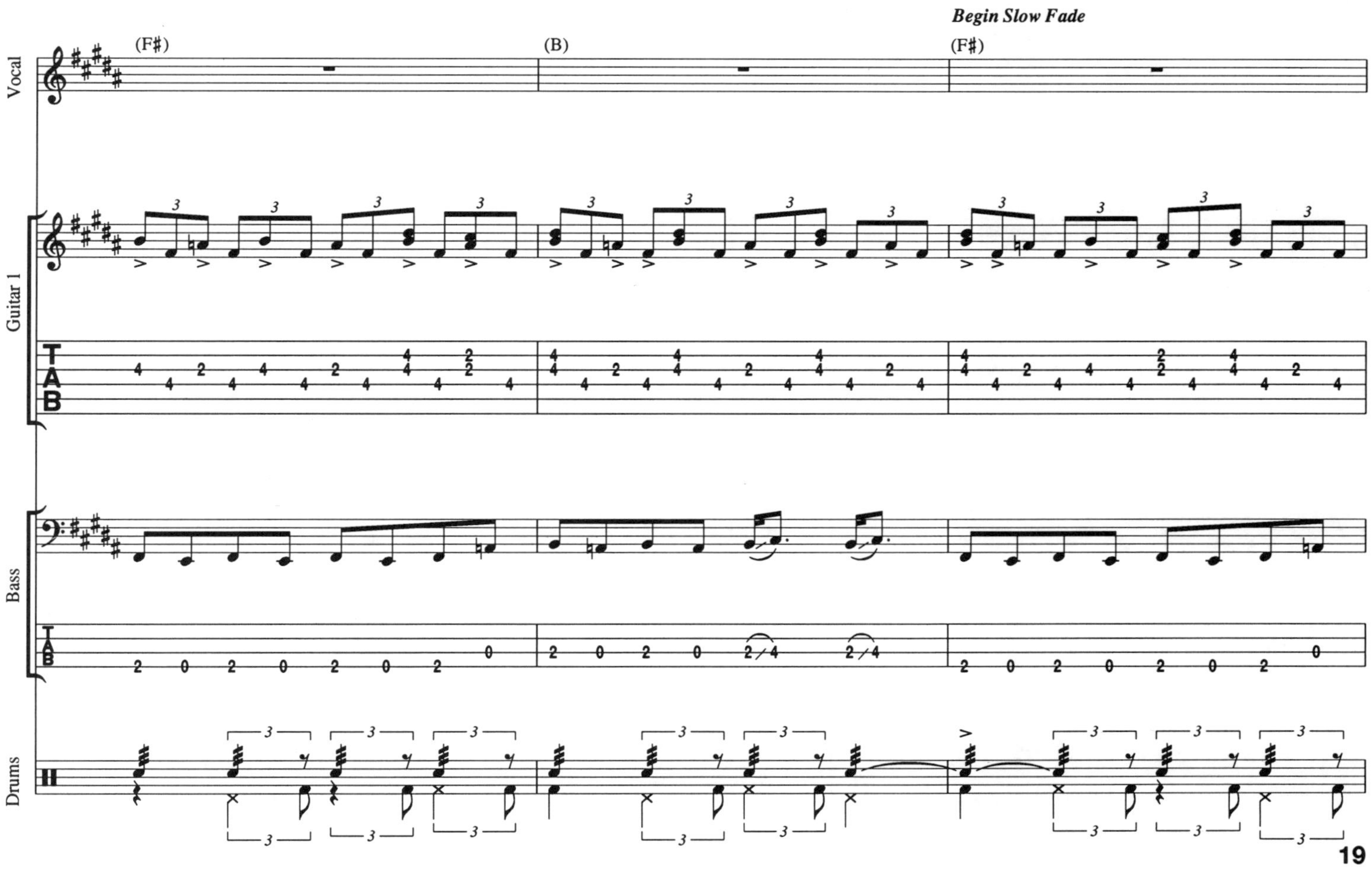
Begin Slow Fade
Vocal
Guitar 1
Bass
Drums
(F♯)
(B)
(F♯)

Aw, shucks.

Spoken: If my dad-dy could see me now.

Vocal
Guitar 1
Bass
Drums
(B)
(F#)
(B)
Ev - 'ry - thing,
ev - 'ry -
grad. bend
grad. release
1 1/2
2
2
2
1 1/2
1/2
Fade Out
(F#)
(B)
(F#)
thing,
ev - 'ry - thing,
oo, ev - 'ry - thing.
full
full
full
1/4
tr

Spanish Castle Magic

Words and Music by Jimi Hendrix

Many of Jimi's compositions were written in key signatures not normally associated with rock music. This one, for instance, is in C# minor, an apt choice, since it allows the main riff's lowest note, the flatted third, to be played on the open sixth and the open first and second strings to be used in conjunction with the C#7#9.

The chromatic progression is also fairly avant-garde for the rock idiom, but Hendrix always had a penchant for the unusual and strived to avoid blatant musical cliches. Examine any of his solos and you'll find at least one little twist or a variation on a familiar theme. Note that in "Spanish Castle Magic"'s guitar solo section there is an abundance of uncommonly bent notes, starting with a minor third bend from C# to E in the first measure at beat 4. Jimi then does some novel double-stop bends, especially the last one. There's simply a wealth of ideas to glean from this solo, so learn it verbatim and then incorporate these "gems" into your lead breaks.

Copyright © 1968, 1977 by EXPERIENCE HENDRIX, L.L.C.
Copyright Renewed 1996
All Rights Controlled and Administered by EXPERIENCE HENDRIX, L.L.C.
All Rights Reserved

Verse
Piano tacet

1. It's ver-y far a-way. It takes a-bout a half a day to get there if we trav-el by my, uh, drag-on-fly.

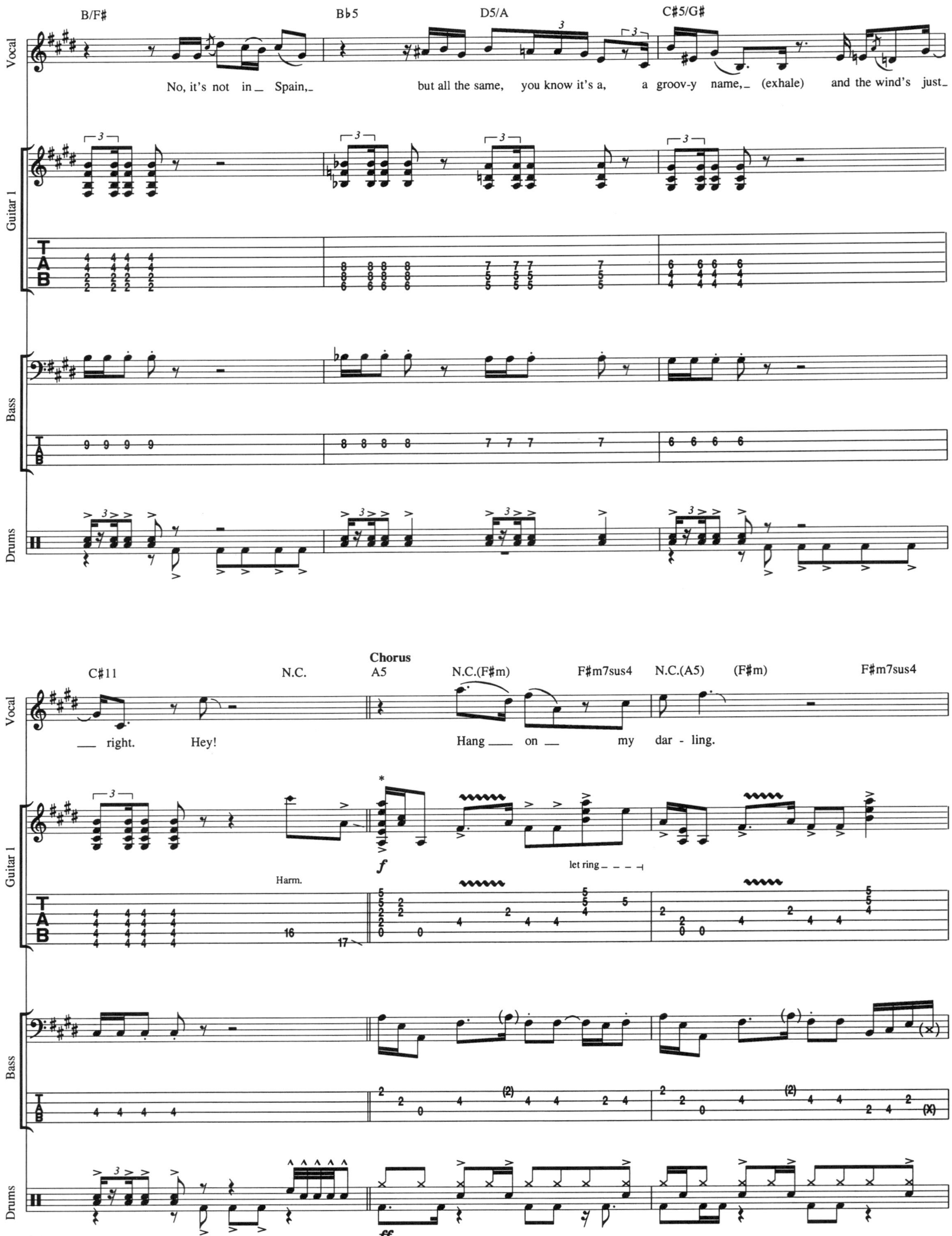

*Doubled simile by piano at this point.

N.C.(E5) (C#7#9) (E5) (C#7#9) (G#m7)
Vocal
Hang on ___ if you want to go. ___
Here, it's a real-ly groov-y place,_ it's a,
Guitar 1
Bass
Drums
(E) (E5) (C#7#9) (E5) (C#7#9)
uh, just a lit-tle bit of, said, uh, Span - ish cast - le mag - ic. ___ Yeah.

Verse
Piano tacet

2. The clouds are really low, and they overflow with cotton candy, and battle grounds, red and brown. But it's all in your mind, don't think your time on

*T – Thumb on ⑥

Chorus
C#5/G#
N.C.
*A5
N.C.(F#m)
Vocal
bad _ things, just float your lit-tle mind a - round. _ Look out! Ooh! Hang _ on ____ my
Guitar 1
Bass
Drums
*Doubled simile by piano till end of song.
(A5) (F#m) (E5) (C#7#9) (E5) (C#7#9)
dar - ling. Yeah! _ Hang on ________ if you want to go. _______ Get up on
full
full
tom fill

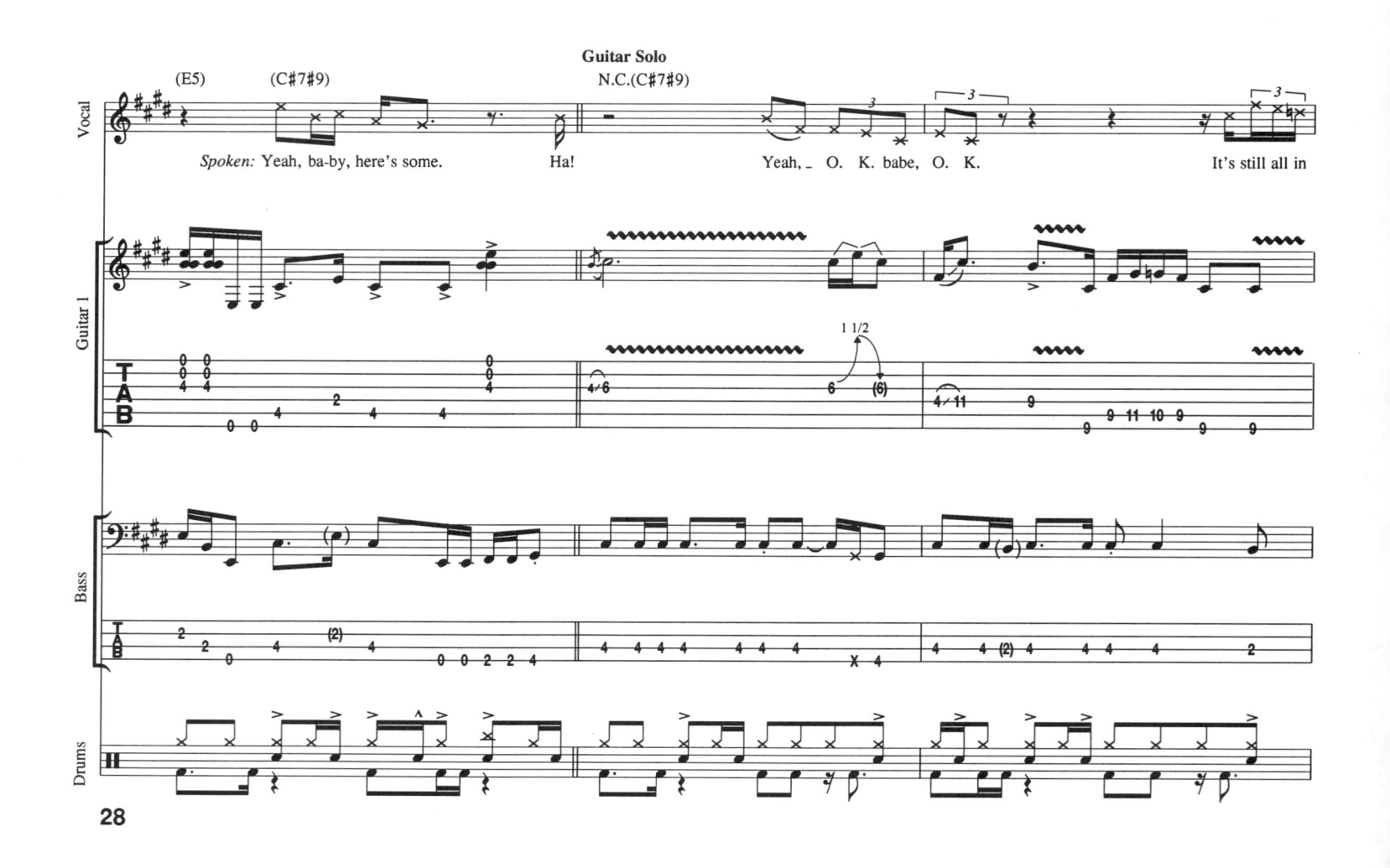

top, real-ly let me groove you, ba-by, with, uh, just a lit-tle bit of Span-ish cas-tle mag-ic.

Spoken: Yeah, ba-by, here's some. Ha! Yeah, O. K. babe, O. K. It's still all in your mind, babe. Ow! Yeah.

*Played behind the beat.
Ah!

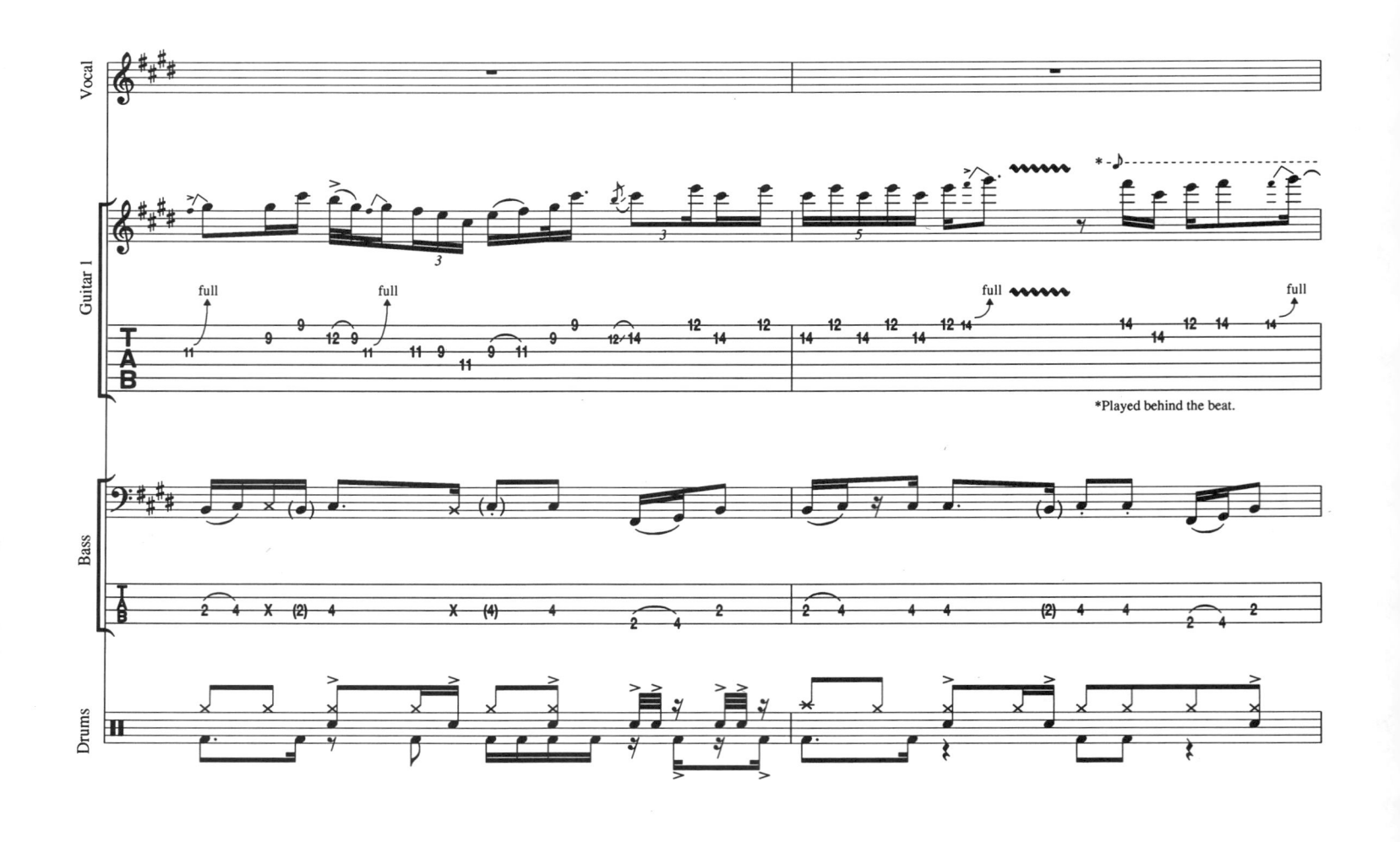

Chorus
A
N.C.(F#m)
A5
N.C.(F#m)
(E5)
(C#7#9)
Vocal
Hang on ___ my dar - ling. ___ Hey! Hang on, hang on if you
Guitar 1
full
full
full
steady gliss.
Bass
Drums

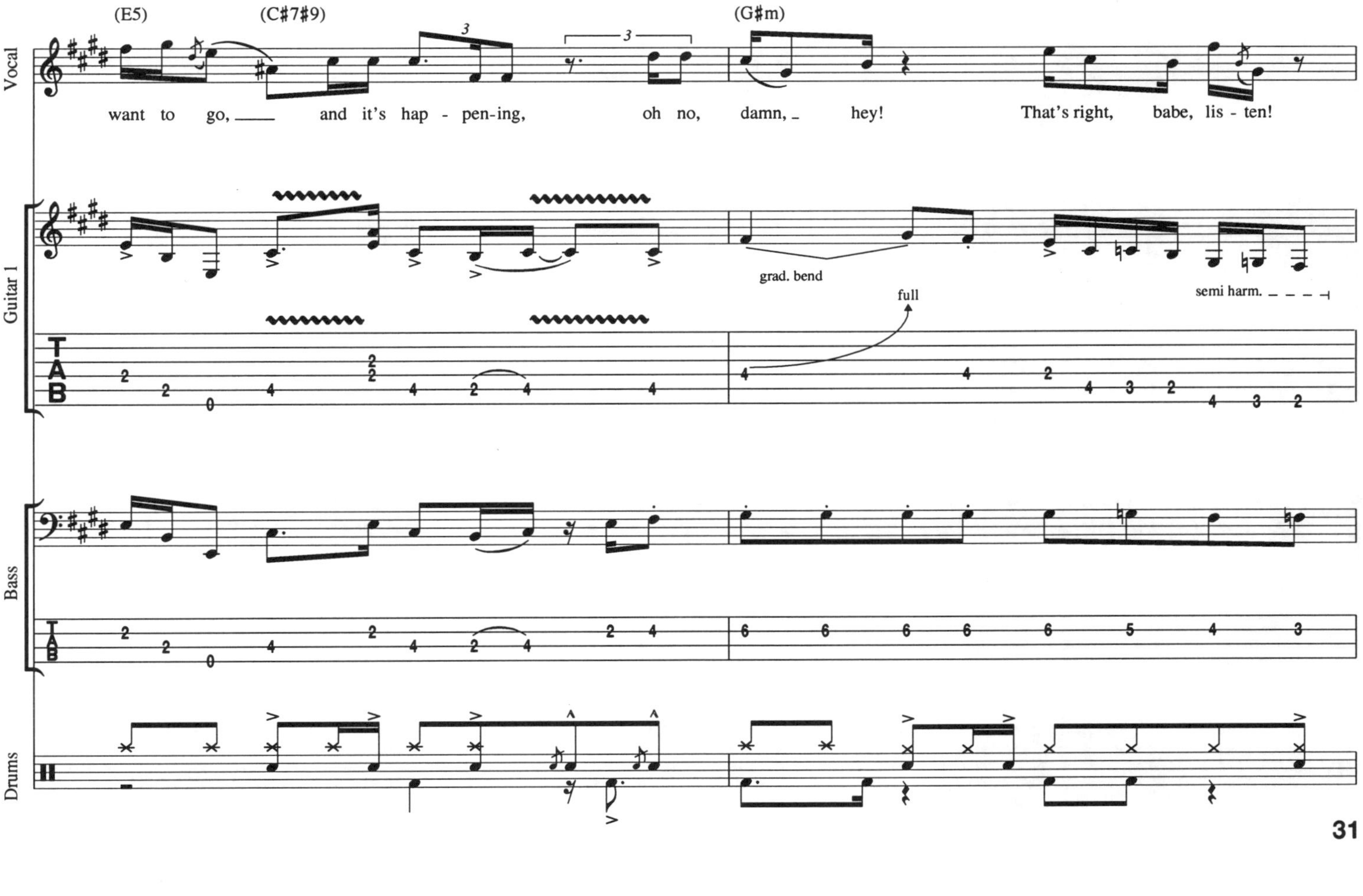
(E5)
(C#7#9)
(G#m)
Vocal
want to go, ___ and it's hap - pen-ing, oh no, damn, _ hey! That's right, babe, lis - ten!
Guitar 1
grad. bend
full
semi harm.
Bass
Drums

32

Vocal
Guitar 1
Bass
Drums
(E) (C#7#9) (E) (C#7#9) (E) (C#7#9)
Get on _ ba-by! Yeah. ___ It's all in your mind, ba-by! Spoken: Lit-tle bit of day dream here and there._
ff
steady gliss.
1/2
full full full full
(E) (C#7#9) (E) (C#7#9)
___ Uh! Yeah!
full full full full full full full 1/2 full

Vocal
Guitar 1
Bass
Drums
(E) (C#7#9) (E) (C#7#9)
Ow!
full 1/2 1/2 1/2 1/2 full full full full full
(E) (C#7#9) (E) (C#7#9) (E) (C#7#9)
Yeah.
Ow!
2 full full full 1 1/2 2 2 2 2 2 full

Ev-'ry-thing's gon-na be al-right!

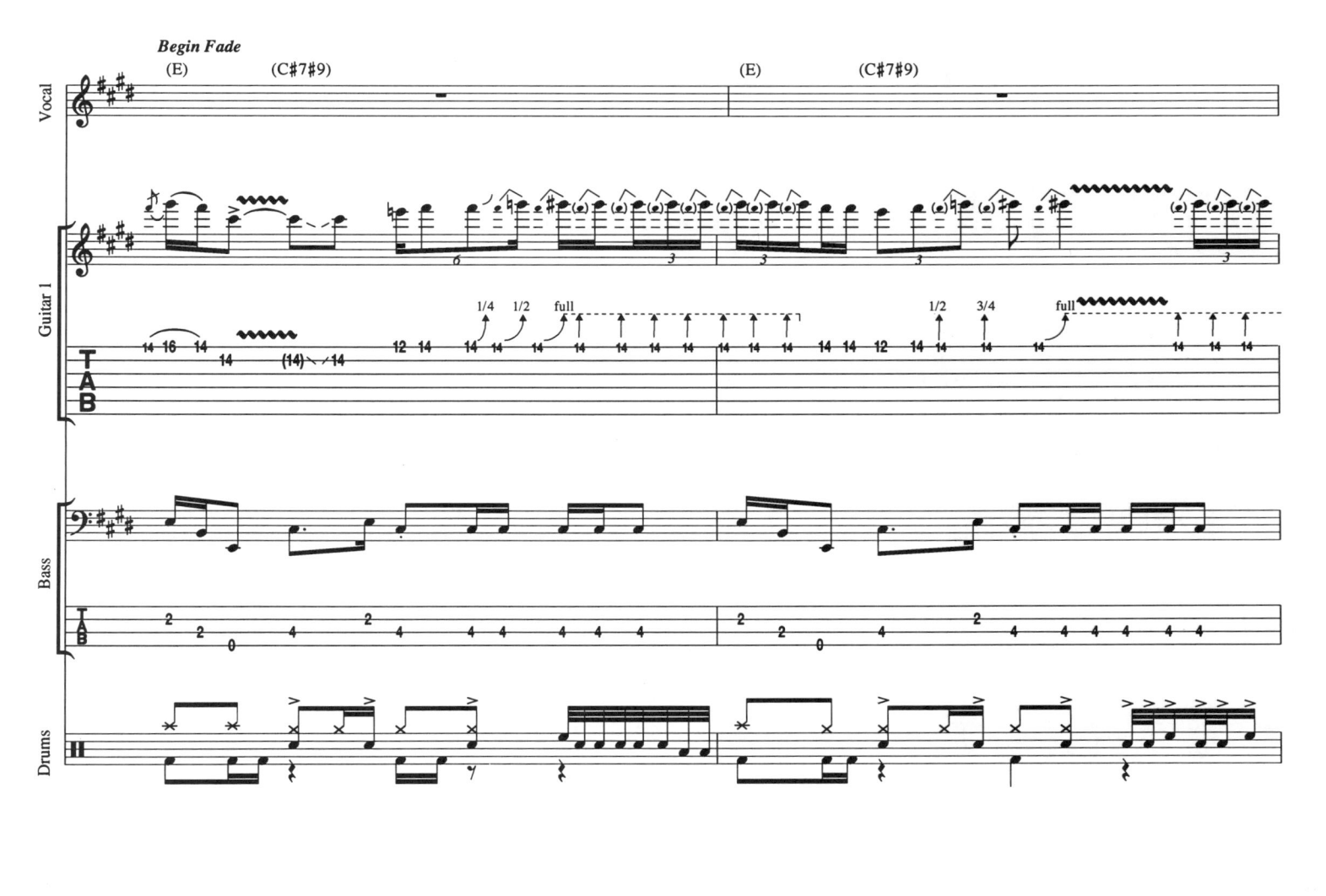

Wait Until Tomorrow

Words and Music by Jimi Hendrix

On the basis of his singular style of storytelling, both in lyric content and accompanying guitar parts, Hendrix could have been the Mark Twain of rock. For instance, note in measure 5 of the third verse that as he queries, "Do I see a silhouette . . ." the guitar seemingly says, "Uh-oh" on beat 3 with the introduction of a G major chord against A in the bass.

The use of pedal point is constant throughout the choruses. While Jimi plays figures based on the progression: I - bIII (E and G major), Noel's part is centered around the tonic. During the first half of this chord cycle he repeatedly plays "sliding sixths," a favorite of Steve Cropper's. This intervallic structure requires the second string to be muffled by the middle finger while it is simultaneously fretting the third string. The same technique is applicable to the playing of octaves, as in "Third Stone From The Sun" off of *Are You Experienced?* and other wide intervals.

Throughout the verses Jimi uses a rather sophisticated concept involving harmonic extensions of the dominant chord built on the fifth degree of a scale, in this case, the major scale. Since the verse modulates to A major, the root of the dominant is an E major triad (E G# B), and by placing a series of thirds above it results in an eleventh chord. Noting that other triads other than E major are within its superstructure of E G# B D F# A, it's possible to take them out of context as Hendrix does commencing with measure 2 of each verse.

Gtr. 1; Tune Down 1/2 Step:
① = Eb ④ = Db
② = Bb ⑤ = Ab
③ = Gb ⑥ = Eb

Bass; Tune Down 1/2 Step:
① = Gb ③ = Ab
② = Db ④ = Eb

*Only basic tonality represented by chord names due to the degree of chordal ornamentations.

Copyright © 1968, 1977 by EXPERIENCE HENDRIX, L.L.C.
Copyright Renewed 1996
All Rights Controlled and Administered by EXPERIENCE HENDRIX, L.L.C.
All Rights Reserved

1. Well, I'm stand-ing here freez-ing in-side your gold-en gar-den, uh, got my lad-der leaned up a-gainst your wall. To-

night's the night we planned to run away together, come on, Dolly Mae, there's no time to stall. But now you're telling me....

Chorus

...think we bet-ter wait 'til to-mor-row. Hey, yeah,
(I think we bet-ter wait 'til to-mor-row.

hey. I think we bet-ter wait 'til to-mor-row. Girl, what 'chu talk-in' 'bout?

E
Gsus2
E
N.C.
Vocal
Yeah, yeah, yeah._
Got to make sure it's right, so un -
I think we bet-ter wait 'til_ to - mor - row.)
Guitar 1
T T T
Bass
w/ auxillary percussion
drum fill
Drums
E
D/E
til to-mor-row, good-night.
Spoken: Oh,_ what a drag.
*w/ slight P.M.
* next 12 meas.

Verse

2. Oh, Dolly Mae, how can you hang me up this way? Oo, on the phone you said you wanted to run off with me today. Now I'm standing here like some turned down serenading fool,

42

Lyrics:
I think we better wait 'til tomorrow. No, can't wait that long. I think we better wait 'til tomorrow. Oh, no.

Got to make sure it's right, un-til to-mor-row, good night, oh, umm, hmm.

*w/ slight P.M.
* next 14 meas.

Spoken: Let's see if I can talk to this girl a lit-tle bit here. Oo,

steady gliss

44

Verse
A
E11
Vocal
ow! 3. Dol - ly Mae, girl, you must be in - sane, so un -
Guitar 1
Bass
Drums
hi-hat
mf
A
E11
sure of your - self lean - ing from your un - sure win - dow pane.

Lyrics:
Do I see a silhouette of somebody pointing something from a tree?
Click, bang, what a hang, your daddy just shot poor me.
Spoken: And I hear you say,

Chorus
E
Vocal
as I fade a - way. . .
Don't have to wait 'til to -
(We don't have to wait 'til to -
Guitar 1
let ring
1/2 full
Bass
(discontinue P.M.)
Drums
ride
Gsus2
mor - row. Hey!
mor - row.
T T T
E
Don't have to wait 'til to -
We don't have to wait 'til to -

Gsus2
E
Gsus2
Vocal
mor - row. What you say? Wait 'til to - mor - row. It
mor - row. We don't have to wait 'til to - mor - row.)
Guitar 1
T T
T T T
Bass
Drums
E N.C.
E
must not have been right, so for - ev - er, good - night, lis - ten at 'cha.
(We don't have to wait 'til to -
drum fill
tom fill

Gsus2
E
Vocal
Ah! Do I have to wait? Don't have to wait.
mor - row. We don't have to wait 'til to -
Guitar 1
Bass
Drums
Gsus2
E
Vocal
It is a drag on my part.
mor - row. We don't have to wait 'til to -
Guitar 1
Bass
Drums

Gsus2
E
N.C.
Vocal
Don't have to wait, uh.
mor - row.)
Um!
Ah, no!
Guitar 1
T T T
full
Harm.
Bass
Drums
tom fill
f
E
Gsus2
E
(We don't have to wait 'til to - mor - row.
Don't have to wait, don't have to wait.
Yeah!
We don't have to wait 'til to -
T T T
mf

Don't have to wait, don't have to wait. We don't have to wait 'til to-morrow.

Oh, no. (morrow.) *Spoken:* I won't be around tomorrow. Yeah!

E
Gsus2
Vocal
(We don't have to wait 'til to - mor - row.
Don't have to wait.
Guitar 1
hold bend
full
Bass
Drums
Begin Fade
E
Gsus2
Vocal
We don't have to wait 'til to - mor - row.
Good - bye, bye, bye!
Guitar 1
Bass
Drums

53

Ain't No Telling

Words and Music by Jimi Hendrix

Beginning with the "call and response" opening, you'll note there is some marvelous interplay between the guitars in this song, especially during the bridge and the instrumental interlude that follows. Throughout the bridge, guitar 1 repeats an ostinato pattern consisting of the tonic and supertonic, C# and D#, while guitar 2 "walks" with the bass. This is followed by what might be viewed as a brief modulation to the distant key of A major for the duration of a four measure contrapuntal instrumental interlude reminiscent of the bridge solo for "The Wind Cries Mary."

As in "Spanish Castle Magic," (which was in C# minor) the use of the dominant seventh with the augmented ninth, Jimi's favorite altered chord, gives this song a major/minor ambiguity since the raised ninth is enharmonic to the minor third.

Copyright © 1968 by EXPERIENCE HENDRIX, L.L.C.
Copyright Renewed 1996
All Rights Controlled and Administered by EXPERIENCE HENDRIX, L.L.C.
All Rights Reserved

Verse
C#7#9
Vocal
ain't no, (Ain't no.) ain't no tell - in' ba - by, when you will
Guitar 1
loco
1/2
Guitar 2
Bass
Drums
E Eadd9 E F# F#add9 F# N.C.(B) (B#) C#7#9 N.C.
see me a - gain, but I pray it will be to - mor - row. 2. Well, the
ride
hi-hat (half open)

Verse
C#7#9
Vocal
sun - rise (Sun - rise.) is burn-in' my eyes ba - by. Well, now I
Guitar 1
1/2
Guitar 2
Bass
Drums
ride
hi-hat (half open)
E Eadd9 E F# F#add9 F# N.C.(B) (B#) C#7#9 N.C. D7
must leave now, but I real-ly hope to see you to - mor - row.
let ring

Bridge
C#7/G#
D7
C#7
N.C.
Vocal
Yeah.
Spoken: Well, my house is, oh, such a sad mile a-way.
Guitar 1
8va
full
full
full
Guitar 2
Bass
Drums
ride
hi-hat (half open)
ride
The feel - in' there al - ways hangs up my day.
Oh, Cle - o - pa - tra, she's

drivin' me insane, she's tryin' to put my body in her brain.

So, uh, just uh, kiss me good-bye, just to ease the pain.

59

Verse

C#7#9

3. Ain't no, _____ ain't no tellin', ba-by. There ain't no tellin', ba-by,
(Ain't no, _____ ain't no tell - in' babe.)

E Eadd9 E F# F#add9 F# N.C.(B) (B#) C#7#9

when you're gon-na see me, 'cause I real-ly hope that, ah, it-'ll be to-mor-row. You know what I'm

E Eadd9 E F♯ F♯add9 F♯ N.C.(B) (B♯)
Vocal
talk - in' 'bout.
(Ain't no tell - in'.)
Woah, yeah,
hope it - 'll be, ah, hope it - 'll be to -
Guitar 1
full
steady gliss.
Guitar 2
Bass
Drums
rivet cym.
C♯7♯9 N.C.(E) (F♯) (B) (B♯)
mor-row.
Ain't no
(Ain't no tell - in'.)
tell - in', ba - by.
Yeah.
You know what I'm

Outro
C#7#9
E Eadd9 E
F# F#add9 F# N.C.(B)
(B#)
Vocal
talk-in' a-bout. An-y-way, must leave now.
Guitar 1
full full
Guitar 2
Bass
Drums
C#7#9
rit.
* w/ echo
w/ bar
* Slap back echo w/ regeneration set high.

Little Wing

Words and Music by Jimi Hendrix

Jimi's protean imagination is evident in his unique chordal style, particularly in a ballad like "Little Wing." In this context, his approach to the guitar is more like that of a pianist: Jimi breaks away from the confines of the dogmatic "rhythm or lead" method. His thumb frets the bass notes, functioning in almost the same manner as a keyboardist's left hand, and the fingers of his fretting hand can be likened to a pianist's right hand. Let's examine a few excerpts that demonstrate this piano style format and rediscover what Adrian Belew has called a "lost art."

On the first beat of measure 2, Jimi frets the root of the G major chord with his thumb, allowing it to be sustained as he follows up with the chord melody. Although the melody is within the third position form of G major, the complete chord is not fingered at any one time. Jimi usually plays dyads (double stops) and movement within these partial chords is oblique; that is one pitch is stationary. If you examine measure 6 you'll find extensive use of oblique motion.

Going to the second verse, an example of parallel motion can be found in measure 2, as the interval of a fourth is slid back and forth over a distance of a whole tone. This idea based on the major pentatonic scale also appears in the coda to "The Wind Cries Mary."

The unusual tonal quality of Jimi's guitar is characteristic of the pickup combination known as the "out-of-phase" mode (see text for "One Rainy Wish"). The ethereal effect beginning with measure 6 is the result of playing through a unit associated with organists, the rotating speaker cabinet or "Leslie." Actually, it's the speaker baffle that moves, creating slow or fast vibration on the principle of the Doppler effect.

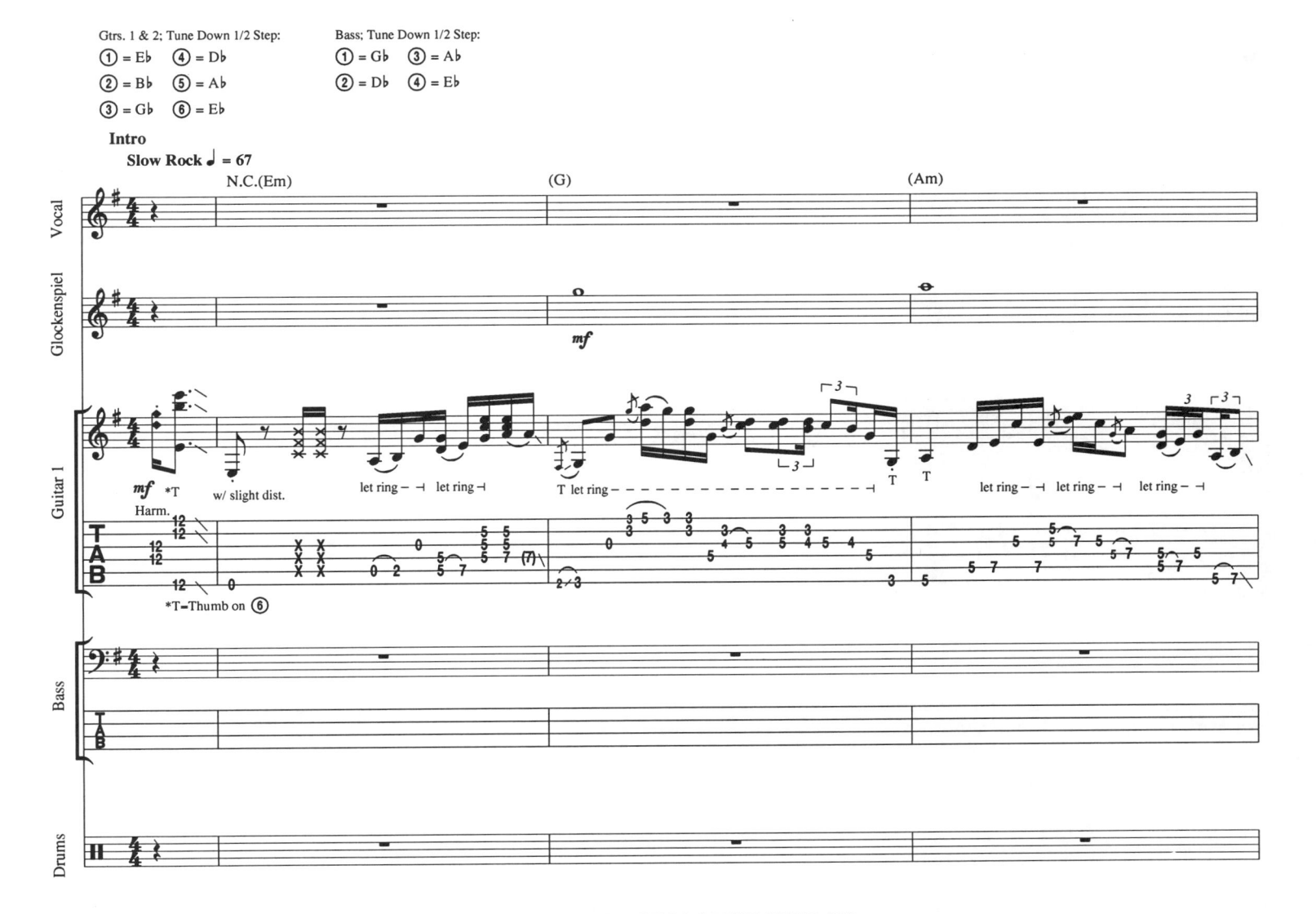

Gtrs. 1 & 2; Tune Down 1/2 Step:
① = E♭   ④ = D♭
② = B♭   ⑤ = A♭
③ = G♭   ⑥ = E♭

Bass; Tune Down 1/2 Step:
① = G♭   ③ = A♭
② = D♭   ④ = E♭

Intro
Slow Rock ♩ = 67

Copyright © 1968 by BELLA GODIVA MUSIC, INC.
This arrangement Copyright © 1995 by BELLA GODIVA MUSIC, INC.
All Rights Controlled and Administered by Don Williams Music Group Inc.
All Rights Reserved   International Copyright Secured

(Em)
(Bm)
(B♭)
(Am)
Vocal
Glockenspiel
Guitar 1
let ring
T
rake
Bass
Drums
(G)
Asus2 Gsus2
Fsus2
N.C.(C6)
(D)
w/ Leslie
mf

D/F#
Verse
N.C.(Em)
(G)
Vocal
1. Well, she's walk-in' through the clouds, with a
Glockenspiel
Guitar 1
T
P.M.
T T T
Bass
mf
w/ pick
hi-hat
Drums
(Am)
(Em)
(Bm)
(B♭)
cir-cus mind that's run-ning wild. But-ter-flies and ze-bras and moon-beams
let ring

(Am)
(G)
(Fadd9)
(C)
Vocal
and, uh, fair - y tales.
That's all she ev-er thinks a-bout.
Rid-ing with the
Glockenspiel
Guitar 1
let ring
Bass
Drums
(D)
D
Verse
N.C.(Em)
wind.
2. When I'm sad she comes to me,

with a thou-sand smiles _ she gives to me _ free.

It's al-right, she says _ it's al-right, _ take an-y-thing _ you want _

68

Am7
Em7
Bm7
B♭
Vocal
Glockenspiel
Guitar 1
full
full
full
full
hold bend
full
full
Guitar 2
Bass
tom fill
Drums

Am
C
D5/A
G
Fadd9
C
Vocal
Glockenspiel
Guitar 1
full
full
full
full
full
Guitar 2
Bass
Drums

Outro
Begin Fade

Yeah, yeah, yeah, yeah,

Fade Out
G
N.C.
Am
N.C.
Em7
Vocal
lit-tle ba - by.
Glockenspiel
8va
loco
Guitar 1
full
full
full
full
full
full
full
Guitar 2
Bass
Drums

If 6 Was 9

Words and Music by Jimi Hendrix

One outstanding feature of this song is that during the verses Jimi doubles his vocal line with the guitar. This device was first used, but to a much lesser extent, in the guitar solo to "Manic Depression" from *Are You Experienced?* There, it was done in unison instead of an octave below his voice, as found here.

Moving along to the bridge, the format switches to chordal accompaniment and the song's momentum builds. Jimi's penchant for lush, complex voicings is evident as he opts to use ninth chords for the first three chords in this descending progression. From a theoretical standpoint, this form naturally occurs when harmonizing on the dominant or fifth degree of a major scale. For example, if we took the D major scale (D E F# G A B C#) and began constructing a chord on A, the fifth degree, by superimposing intervals of a third (tertian harmony), our first true chord would be a major triad consisting of A, C# and E. Continuing in the same manner will result in various harmonic extensions (7, 9, 11 and 13), but for our purposes we'll just require the seventh, G, and then replace the third, C#, with the second, B, to form the ninth.

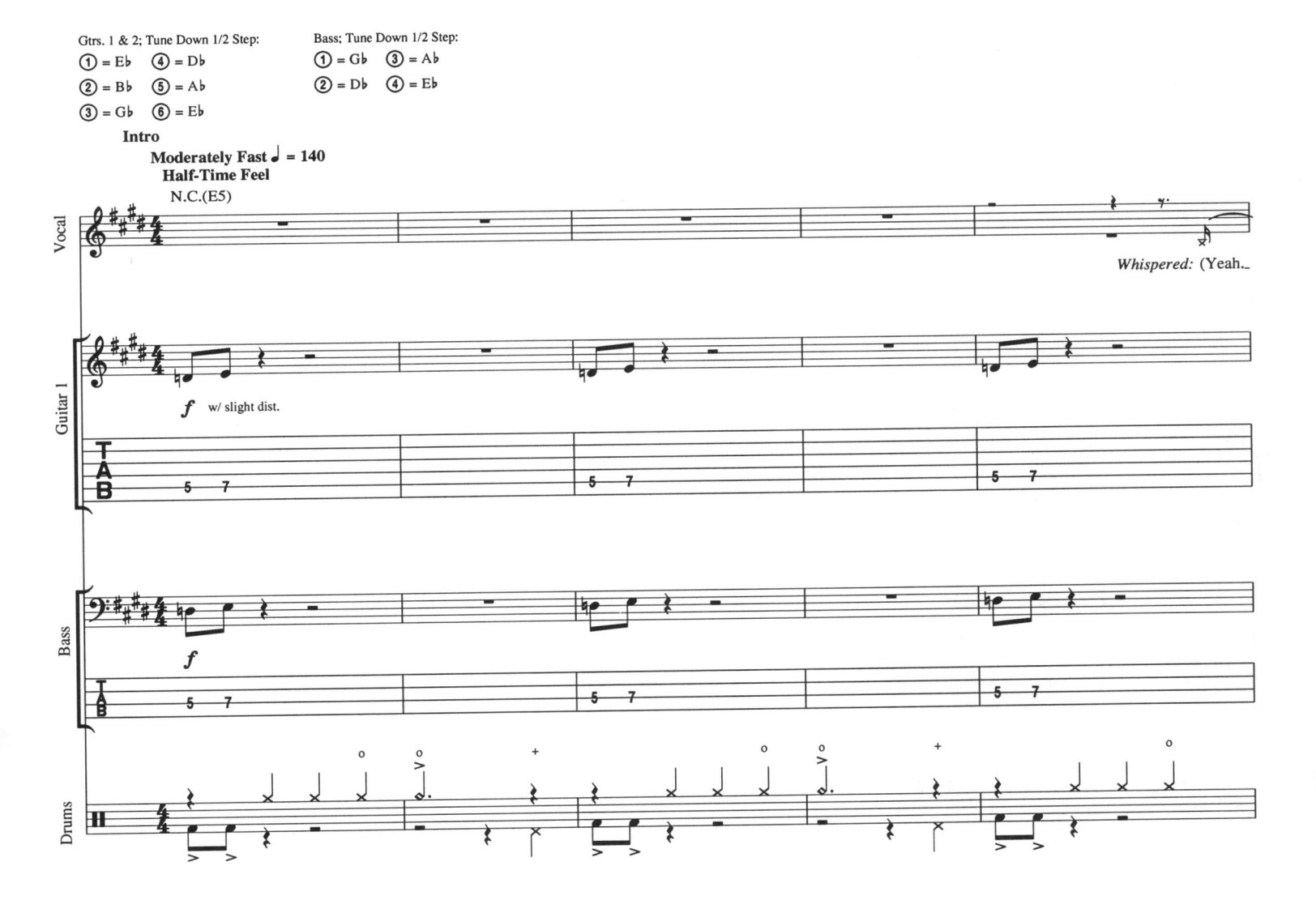

Gtrs. 1 & 2; Tune Down 1/2 Step:
① = Eb   ④ = Db
② = Bb   ⑤ = Ab
③ = Gb   ⑥ = Eb

Bass; Tune Down 1/2 Step:
① = Gb   ③ = Ab
② = Db   ④ = Eb

Intro
Moderately Fast ♩ = 140
Half-Time Feel

74

Lyrics:
_____) If the mountains, _____ ah, fell in the sea, _____ let it be, _____ it ain't me. _____ *Whispered:* (Well, alright.) Got my own _____

End Half-Time Feel

Bridge
A9

*T = Thumb on ⑥

Half-Time Feel
G9
F#9
F
E
N.C.
Vocal
world _ to live through and, a - ha, and I ain't gon - na cop - y you. ______
Guitar 1
full
Bass
Drums
mf
Verse
E
N.C.
E7#9
Yes.
2.Now if a six uh, huh, turned out _ to be
Whispered: (Sing the song bro-ther.)
full

nine, _____ oh, I don't mind. _____ Oh, I don't mind, _____ uh. *Whispered:* (Well, al-

right. _) If all the hip-pies _____ cut off all _ their hair, _____ oh, I don't care. _

End Half-Time Feel
Bridge
D5 E5 N.C.(D5)
D5 E5 N.C.(D5)
A9
Vocal
Oh, I don't care.
Dig.
'Cause I've
got my own
Guitar 1
let ring
T
A
B
Bass
Drums
ride
f
Half-Time Feel
G9
F♯9
F
E
world to live through and, uh,
and I
ain't gon - na cop - y
you.

Interlude
N.C.(E5)
Vocal
Spoken: White col-lar con-ser-va-tive flash-in' down the street point-in' their plas-tic fin-ger at me, ha.
Guitar 1
mf
f
1/2
full
Bass
Drums
press roll
mf
(leave open)
They're hop-in' that soon my kind will drop and die, but, uh, I'm gon-na wave my free flag high,
let ring

Guitar Solo
End Half-Time Feel
E E5
E
C9
Vocal
high!
Ow!
Guitar 1
let ring
Bass
Drums
E6
Guitar 2
8va
mf
w/ echo & clean tone

A9
G9
E6
Vocal
Guitar 1
Guitar 2
Bass
Drums
let ring
8va
rake
tom fill
Wave on, wave on.

82

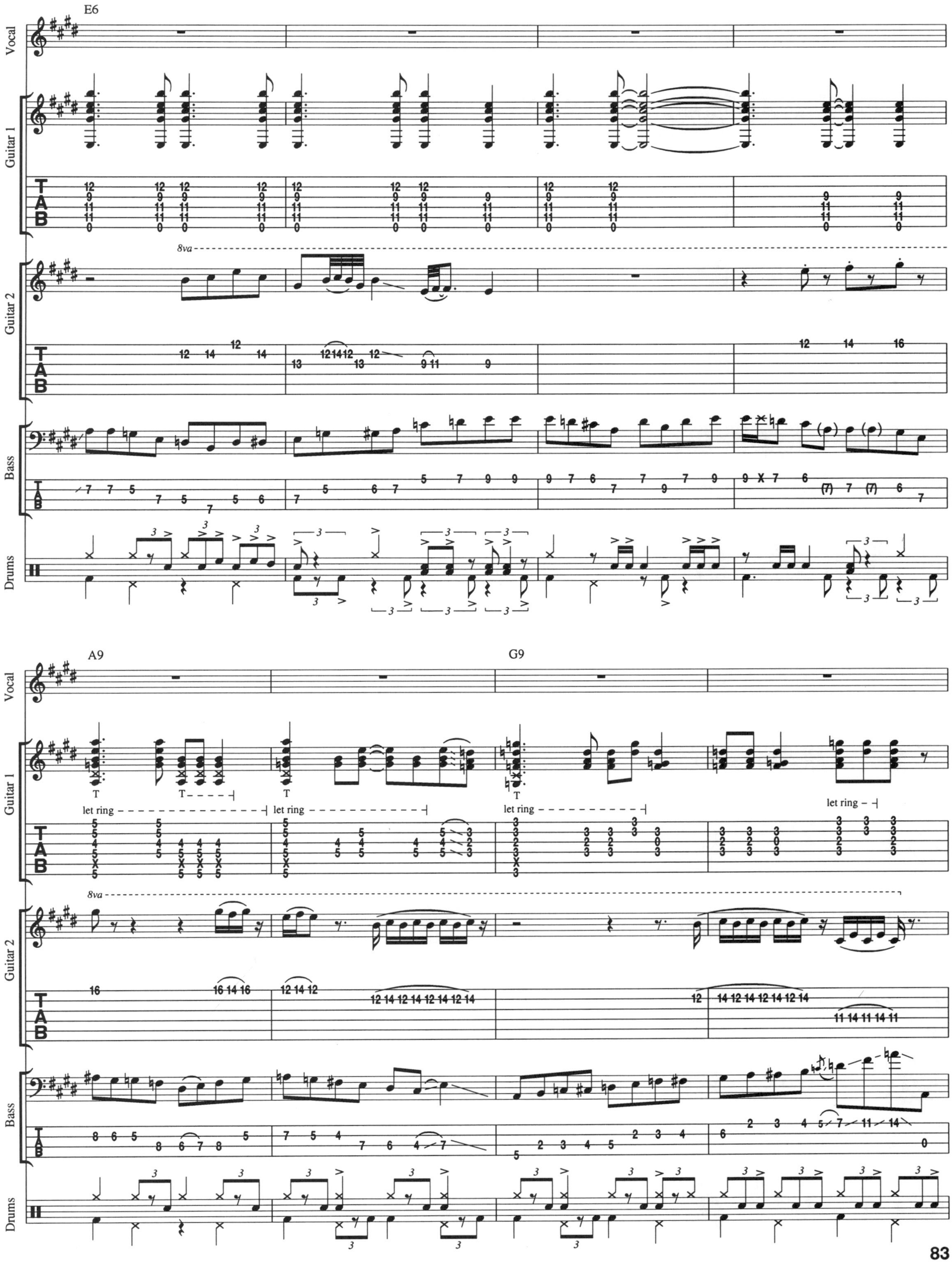
E6
A9
G9
Vocal
Guitar 1
Guitar 2
Bass
Drums
8va
let ring
T

Bm7
N.C.(B5)
B
A5/BBsus2
B9sus4
Vocal
Guitar 1
let ring
Guitar 2
8va
Bass
Drums
B
full

Verse
Half-Time Feel
N.C.(E5)
Vocal
Ah, ha, ha.
Spoken: 3. Fall moun - tains. Just don't fall on me.
Go a-head on mis-ter bus-'ness man, you can't dress like
Guitar 1
Guitar 2
8va
loco
Bass
Drums
choke
hi-hat
tom fill
ride
tom
mf

*Drum Solo

*w/ voc. ad Lib (next 12 meas.)

87

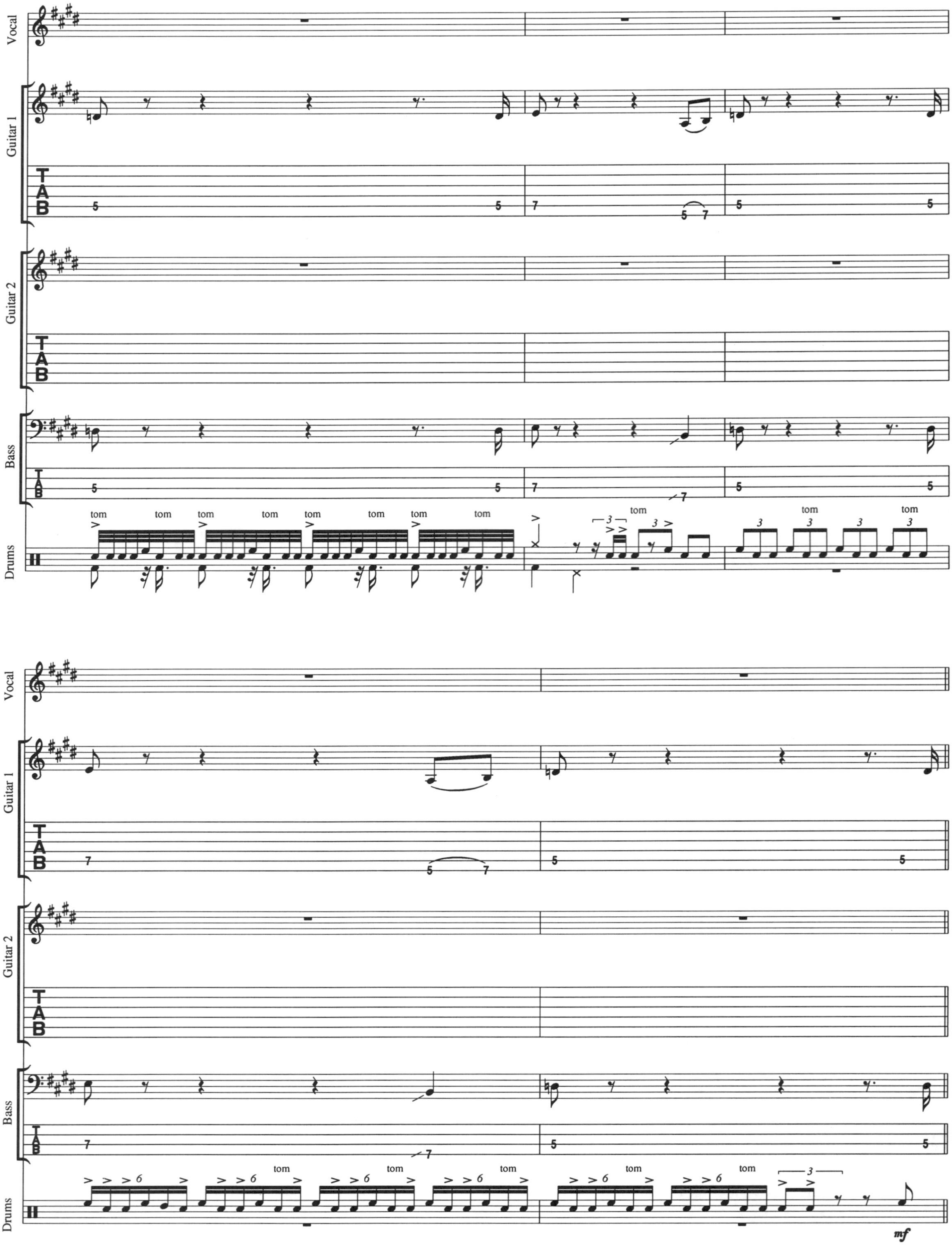
Vocal
Guitar 1
Guitar 2
Bass
Drums
tom
mf

Verse

Spoken: 4. Don't no-bod-y know what I'm talk-in' a-bout?   I've got my own life to live.

I'm the one that's gon-na have to die when it's time for me to die, so let me live my life ... the way I want to. ... There.

Sing on brother, play on drummer.

End Half-Time Feel **Guitar Solo** E^6_9

90

F♯m7/E
E 6/9
Vocal
Guitar 1
Guitar 2
Bass
Drums
8va
toms
E13
E6sus4
B9
E6sus4
let ring

92

Em
E6/9
Emaj7
Vocal
Guitar 1
let ring
Guitar 2
8va
steady gliss.
* Succession of slides w/ fretboard against mic. stand (next 5 meas.)
Bass
Drums
Esus4
w/ Indian flute ad Lib till end of song.
E13
15ma

F♯m7
N.C.(E)
Vocal
Guitar 1
let ring
Guitar 2
8va
Bass
Drums
tom
F♯m7
Emaj7
Emaj9
Vocal
Guitar 1
let ring
Guitar 2
8va
Bass
Drums
tom
tom

F#m7
E
Vocal
Guitar 1
let ring
8va
loco
Guitar 2
Bass
tom fill
Drums
F#m7/E
Emaj9

E
F♯m7
Emaj9 F♯m7
Vocal
8va
Guitar 1
let ring
let ring
Guitar 2
Bass
Drums
E
F♯m7
loco
let ring
8va

Vocal
Guitar 1
Guitar 2
Bass
Drums
Emaj9
F♯m7
Emaj9
8va

Vocal
Guitar 1
Guitar 2
Bass
Drums
F♯m7
Emaj9
Emaj7
8va
loco
let ring

F♯m7
Emaj9
Vocal
Guitar 1
Guitar 2
Bass
Drums
let ring
8va
steady gliss.
let ring
F♯m7
E9
loco
let ring
let ring
loco
ad lib
freely

You Got Me Floatin'

Words and Music by Jimi Hendrix

The opening guitar figure is in "reverse" through manipulation of the tape as on "Are You Experienced?" from the first LP. Check out the accompanying notes to that song for a detailed account of this recording technique and optional methods of replicating the "backwards" effect.

Jimi then shifts into "drive" with the funky main riff, resplendent with sharply attacked partial chords and muted strings. Note that all muting is done by the fretting hand versus the traditional palm mute.

The most notable feature of this cut has to do with its novel instrumentation. An eight-string bass is used in this piece and is prominent in the interlude solo as it is played in counterpoint to the guitar. For those of you unfamiliar to this type of bass, it is similar to the four string variety except for adjunct strings an octave higher to give the effect of a guitar doubling the bass part.

Gtrs. 1 & 2; Tune Down 1/2 Step:
① = E♭   ④ = D♭
② = B♭   ⑤ = A♭
③ = G♭   ⑥ = E♭

†Bass; Tune Down 1/2 Step:
① = G♭   ③ = A♭
② = D♭   ④ = E♭
†8-str. elec. bass

Intro
Freely ♩ = 95

Moderately Fast Rock ♩ = 130

* Backwards guitar.

Copyright © 1968, 1977 by EXPERIENCE HENDRIX, L.L.C.
Copyright Renewed 1996
All Rights Controlled and Administered by EXPERIENCE HENDRIX, L.L.C.
All Rights Reserved

Verse

1. Well, you got me float-in' a - round and 'round.

Al - ways up, you nev - er let me down. The a - maz-ing thing; you turn me on nat' - ral - ly, oh,

Chorus
C D6 C5 N.C. C5 D5 C5 D5 C5 N.C.
N.C.(C) (D) N.C. (C) (A) N.C.
and I kiss you when I please.
We're float - in' 'round and 'round.
(You got me float - in' 'round and 'round. You
(C) (D) N.C. (C) (A) N.C. (C) (D) N.C. (C) (A) N.C.
Hey! Touch the ceil-ing, babe. Got me float - in' nat - 'ral-ly.
got me float - in', nev - er down. You got me float - in', nat' - ral - ly. You
Vocal
Guitar 2
Guitar 1
Bass
Drums

Verse
(C) (D) N.C. (C) (A) N.C. C D C N.C. C5 D5 C Gsus4 N.C. C5 D5
Vocal
Yeah! 2. Now ya, ya got me float-in' a - cross_ and through._ You
got me float - in', float_ to please.)
Guitar 2
Guitar 1
Bass
Drums
C D C N.C. G5 A5 C Gsus4 C5 D5 C D C N.C. G5 A5 C5 Gsus4 N.C. G5 A5
make me float right on out_ to you. There's on - ly one thing I need to real - ly get a me there,_ is to
1/4

Chorus
C D C N.C. G5 A5 C D5 C5 N.C. N.C.(C) (D) N.C. (C) (A) N.C.
hear you laugh with-out a care. What I say now, ah. Hey! Huh, 'round and 'round.
(You got me float - in' 'round and 'round. You
(C) (D) N.C. (C) (A) N.C. (C) (D) N.C. (C) (A) N.C.
Got me float - in'. Whoa, hey! Got me float - in' nat - 'ral - ly.
got me float - in', nev - er down. You got me float - in', nat' - ral - ly. You
Vocal
Guitar 2
Guitar 1
Bass
Drums
full
1/2

Interlude
(C) (D) N.C. (C) (A) N.C.
A7
Vocal
Float - in'.
got me float - in', float ___ to please. _)
Got _ me float - in'.
Guitar 2
Guitar 1
Bass
Drums
hi-hat
ride
*Octavia pedal generates additional pitch one octave higher
(next 16 meas.).
Ooh.

105

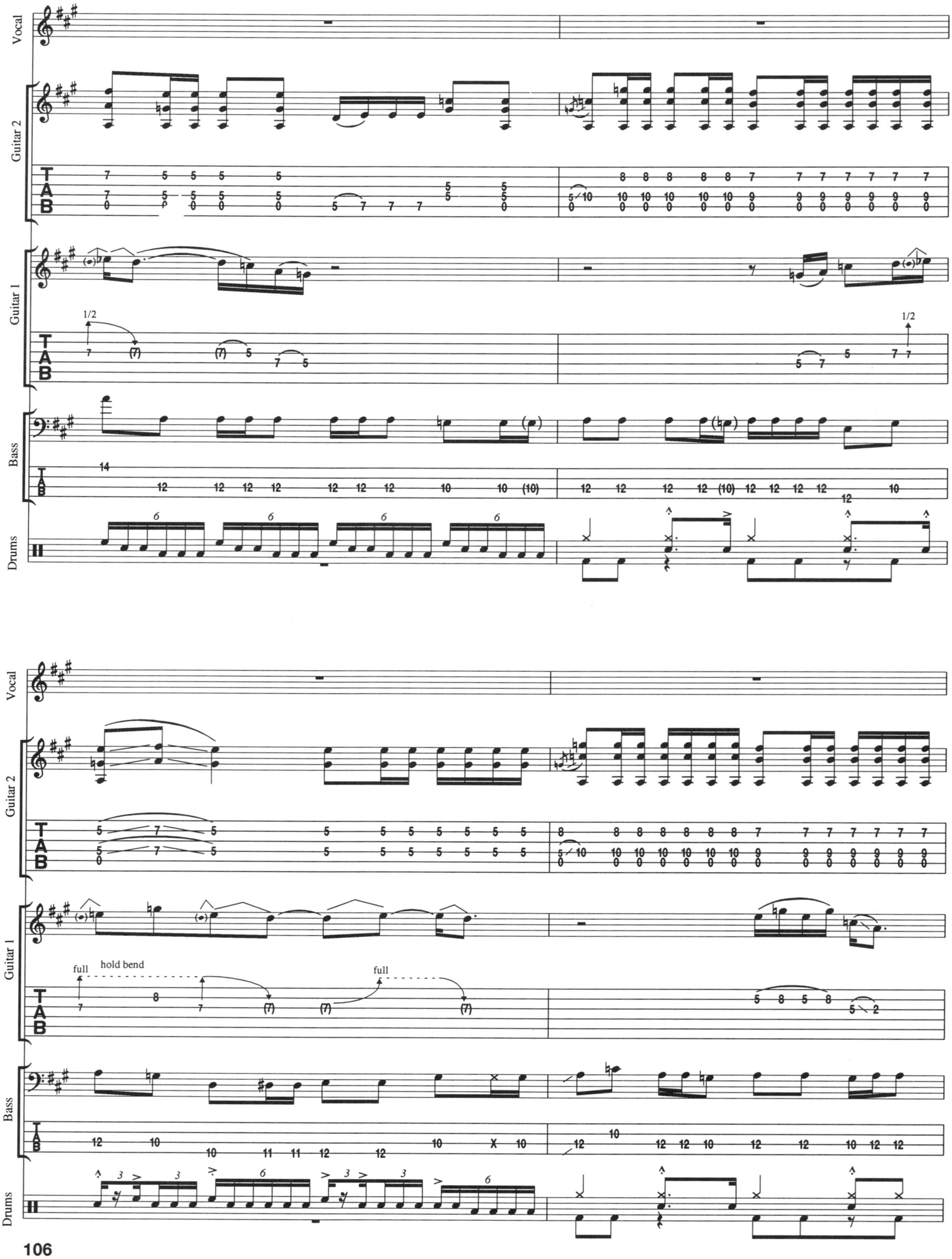
Vocal
Guitar 2
Guitar 1
Bass
Drums
1/2
full
hold bend

Chorus

Yeah! Got me float-in' 'round and 'round. Gim-me one more time, broth-er, say it. You

(C) (D) N.C. (C) (A) N.C. (C) (D) N.C.
Vocal
Got me float - in', yeah. See the sky?
Vocal
got me float - in', nev-er down. You've got me float - in',
Guitar 2
Guitar 1
8va
1/2
steady gliss.
Bass
Drums
(C) (A) N.C. (C) (D) N.C. (C) (A) N.C.
Look up. 3. Now, your
nat - 'ral - ly. You got me float - in', float to please.
loco
8va
1/2
1/2
1/2
steady gliss.

dad-dy's cool and your mom-ma's no fool. They both know I'm heads o-ver heels for you. And when the day it melts down in-to a sleep-y, red glow, that's

Lyrics:
when my de-sires ___ start to show. ___

Outro:
Have ___ me float-in'. Hey! ___ Hey! ___ You

N.C.
A9
Bb9/A
A9
N.C. C9
Vocal
Got me float - in'.
Voc. Fig. 1
Touch the
got me float - in'.
You got me float - in'.
Guitar 2
Guitar 1
Bass
Drums
full
1/2
A9
Bb9/A
w/ Voc. Fig. 1, 5 times
A9
N.C.
A9
Bb9/A
sky.
End Voc. Fig. 1
You got me float - in'.
You
steady gliss.
8va

A9
N.C.
A9
N.C.
B♭9/A
N.C.
G9/A
Vocal
Hey, hey, hey, hey, now, hey - o.
Guitar 2
Guitar 1
8va
1/2
Bass
Drums
A9
N.C.
A9
N.C.
A9
B♭9/A
Float - in', hey, hey!
loco
full
8va

Begin Fade
A9 A13 A9 A13 A9 B♭9/A
Vocal
Ow!
Hey!
Guitar 2
Guitar 1
8va
Bass
Drums
A9 N.C. A9 B♭9/A A9
Fade Out
Got me float-in'.

Castles Made Of Sand

Words and Music by Jimi Hendrix

Whereas Jimi's anthem to nonconformity, "If 6 Was 9," was vehemently subjective in its declarations, here he is more or less a detached observer of life's ironies. There's even a certain pathos to the music itself which can be attributed to the fact that there are brief departures from the major mode to minor.

The first voicing, G5add 9 (also called Gsus2) has a rather bittersweet quality to it, being neither "fish nor fowl" (i.e. major nor minor), and then B♭, the minor third, is introduced by virtue of the parallel movement of the opening chordal figure and its recapitulation at the song's conclusion. Note also that the minor mode is inferred by the entrance of a B♭ major chord in the last measures of the introduction.

As in "You Got Me Floating," there's that ubiquitous "backwards" guitar in the background, and this time it is also the solo instrument.

Memorization of this song is a must for any guitar-slinging Hendrix devotee. Just ask Frank Marino of Mahogany Rush fame, an "honor student" of the Jimi Hendrix school of guitar.

Gtrs. 1 & 2; Tune Down 1/2 Step:
① = E♭ ④ = D♭
② = B♭ ⑤ = A♭
③ = G♭ ⑥ = E♭

Bass; Tune Down 1/2 Step:
① = G♭ ③ = A♭
② = D♭ ④ = E♭

Copyright © 1968, 1977 by EXPERIENCE HENDRIX, L.L.C.
Copyright Renewed 1996
All Rights Controlled and Administered by EXPERIENCE HENDRIX, L.L.C.
All Rights Reserved

Slower ♩ = 92
N.C.
(Bm7)
(Gsus2)
(Am7)
(Fsus2)
(B♭5)
Vocal
Guitar 1
let ring
A.H.
pitch: D
let ring
let ring
Guitar 2
Bass
Drums
G
N.C.
(B♭)
(C)
G
N.C.
(B♭)
(C)
Verse
Fsus2
1. Down the street you can hear her scream, "You're a dis - grace," as she
let ring
let ring
let ring
mf
w/ pick
f

slams the door in his drunk-en face. And now he stands out - side and all the neigh-bors start to gos-sip and drool. He cries, "Oh girl, you must be mad. What hap-pened to the sweet love you and me had?" A-gainst the door he leans and starts a scene, and his tears fall and burn the gar-den green.

118

war games in the woods with his Indian friends. And he built a dream that when he grew up he would be a fearless warrior Indian Chief. Man-y moons passed and more the dream grew strong until to-morrow he would sing his first _____ war song, and fight his first bat-tle, but some-thing went wrong. Sur-prise at-tack _ killed him in his sleep _ that night.

Chorus

Lyrics: And so castles made of sand _____ melts into the sea, eventually. _____

Guitar Solo

N.C.(Gm7)
(C)
(G)
(B♭)
(C)
Vocal
Guitar 1
Guitar 2
Bass
Drums
full
1/2
8va
3. There

Verse

Fsus2 ... A5
was a young girl whose heart was a frown. 'cause she was crip-pled for life and she could-n't speak a sound. And she

Em7 ... F6sus2 C G5 N.C.(G5)
wished and prayed she could stop liv-in', so she de-cid-ed to die.

Lyrics: She drew her wheel-chair to the edge of the shore, and to her legs she smiled, "You won't hurt me no more." But then a sight she'd nev-er seen made her jump and say,

"Look, a gold-en winged ship is pass-ing my way." *Spoken:* And it real-ly did-n't

Outro
Freely ♩ = 80

have to stop, it just kept on go-ing. And so cas-tles

Vocal
Guitar 1
Guitar 2
Bass
Drums
(Am7)
(B♭5)
(G)
N.C.(B♭)
(C)
made of sand
slips in-to the sea,
e-
G
N.C.(B♭)
(C)
ven-tu-al-ly.
G
N.C.(B♭)
(C)
rit.
rit.
T
T

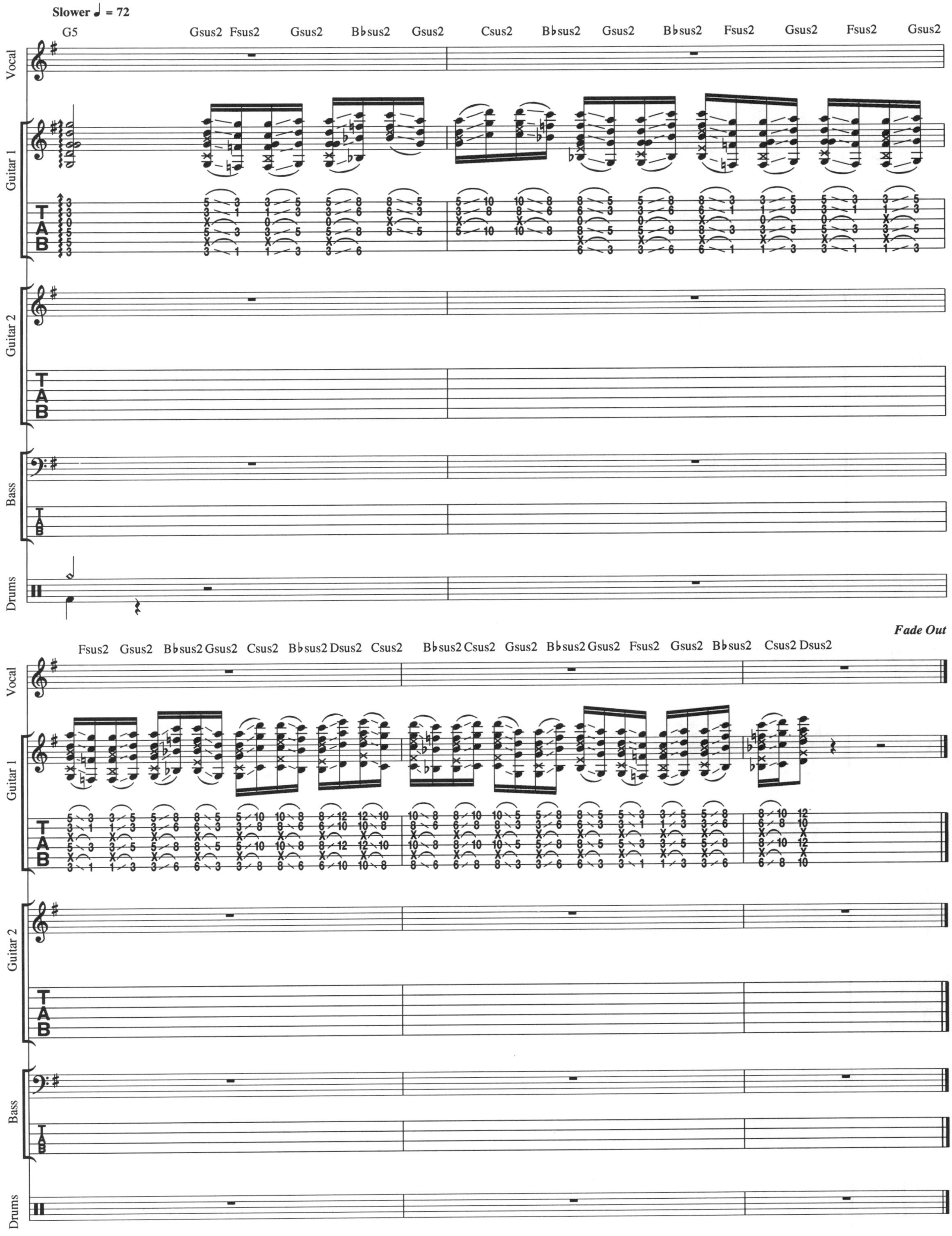
Slower ♩ = 72
G5
Gsus2 Fsus2 Gsus2 B♭sus2 Gsus2
Csus2 B♭sus2 Gsus2 B♭sus2 Fsus2 Gsus2 Fsus2 Gsus2
Vocal
Guitar 1
Guitar 2
Bass
Drums
Fade Out
Fsus2 Gsus2 B♭sus2 Gsus2 Csus2 B♭sus2 Dsus2 Csus2
B♭sus2 Csus2 Gsus2 B♭sus2 Gsus2 Fsus2 Gsus2 B♭sus2
Csus2 Dsus2

She's So Fine

Words and Music by Noel Redding

Noel Redding made his songwriting and lead vocal debut on *Axis: Bold As Love* with this composition. Decidedly in a psychedelic pop vein, this song is based primarily on the A Mixolydian mode (A B C# D E F# G), which differs from the major scale or Ionian mode in that the seventh degree is lowered. One exception is in the verses when D is the temporary tonal center, as in measures 15-18; at this point in the progression the D Mixolydian (D E F# G A B C) replaces the A.

Throughout the verses, Jimi's fills are either derived from the A major pentatonic scale (A B C# E F#) or the aforementioned Mixolydian modes. The interlude is in G and the lead follows the G major pentatonic scale with the addition of the fourth (G A B C D E).

As far as technique goes, the only sections you may experience a bit of difficulty with are where two adjacent strings are bent in parallel fashion, as in, for example, measures 21-22. This bend will require particular attention to intonation as well as some strong fingers.

Gtrs. 1 & 2; Tune Down 1/2 Step:
① = Eb   ④ = Db
② = Bb   ⑤ = Ab
③ = Gb   ⑥ = Eb

Bass; Tune Down 1/2 Step:
① = Gb   ③ = Ab
② = Db   ④ = Eb

Intro

Moderate Rock ♩ = 132

*Key signature denotes A Mixolydian.

Copyright © 1967 by Joint Music Co.
Copyright Renewed
All Rights Administered by Chappell & Co.
International Copyright Secured   All Rights Reserved

Vocal
Guitar 1
Guitar 2
Bass
Drums
loco
1/2
full
f w/ clean tone
tom fill
1. She
Verse
A5 A5/G A5/F♯ A5/E A5 A5/G A5/F♯ A5/E
walks with a bell clock 'round her neck so the hip - pies think she's in with time.

Her hair glis-tens like rob-ins on a deck. Branch-es at-tacked me from her neck. She's so (She's so

131

rain from a tree soaks in-to her mind. (Mind.

D5 C5 D5 D C5 B5 C5 B5 D5 C5 B5 C5 B5 N.C.

Morn-ing signs sound just like a lark, all these signs are al-ways the start.

Chorus
Bridge
A
G
N.C.
A5
D5
D6
She's so fine.
(She's so fine.
She's so
very - y, ver - y fine.
When I veer I
Oo,
let ring
full
tom fill
Vocal
Guitar 1
Guitar 2
Bass
Drums

E5 E6 E7 D5 D6 D5 D6 D5 E5 E6 E7 D5 D6 D5 D6 D5 D6 D5
Vocal
get so near, but so far, far, far a - way. Lis - ten to
Vocal
la. Oo, la. Oo.
(La, la, la.) (La, la, la.)
Guitar 1
Guitar 2
Bass
Drums
tom fill
E5 E
E5
me to - day.
Oo.
(La, la, la.) (La, la, la, la, la, la, la, la, la, la, la, la, la, la, la.,
tom fill
tom fill

Interlude

(la, la, la, la, la, la, la, la.)

136

N.C.
D C D C D C
Vocal
She's so fine.
)
Guitar 1
full
full
Guitar 2
Bass
Drums
tom fill
D5
A
E5
Fine.
(Fine.
1/4
tom fill

138

N.C.(A5)
A7
A6
N.C.
(A5)
A7
A6
N.C.
Vocal
Guitar 1
full
full
full
Guitar 2
Bass
let ring
let ring
Drums
tom fill
A5
A5/G
A5
D/F#
rit.
w/ bar
-1/2
w/ bar
slack
rit.
w/ bar
-1
slack
rit.

One Rainy Wish

Words and Music by Jimi Hendrix

Another of Jimi's "Honor Students," Eric Johnson, cites this ode to a dream as one of his personal favorites. It's also near the top of my list, primarily for its aesthetic appeal, but it has a sufficient amount of radical Hendrixian harmonic and rhythmic concepts to warrant some lengthy academically-minded musings.

To my knowledge, this was the first rock song to have the verse and chorus in different time signatures. Up 'til the last measure of the first verse it is in triple meter, 3/4 time, which is then replaced by the double meter, 4/4 time, of the chorus.

The harmonies contain numerous Jimi signatures, most notably by guitar 2 starting with the opening E6 chord and harmonization of the E major pentatonic scale (E F# G# B C#) in fourths, commencing with measure 6 to the exquisite A major add 9 voicing in the second measure of the verse. The guitar also has a decidedly "nasal" quality to it, due to the fact that the bridge and middle pickups were engaged simultaneously. This was before the advent of five-way pickup selectors on Stratocasters and Jimi attained this setting - erroneously dubbed by most as the "out-of-phase" mode - by first removing the spring from its precursor, the three-way switch. This setting is also employed in "Castles Made Of Sand," "Wait Until Tomorrow" and "Ain't No Telling."

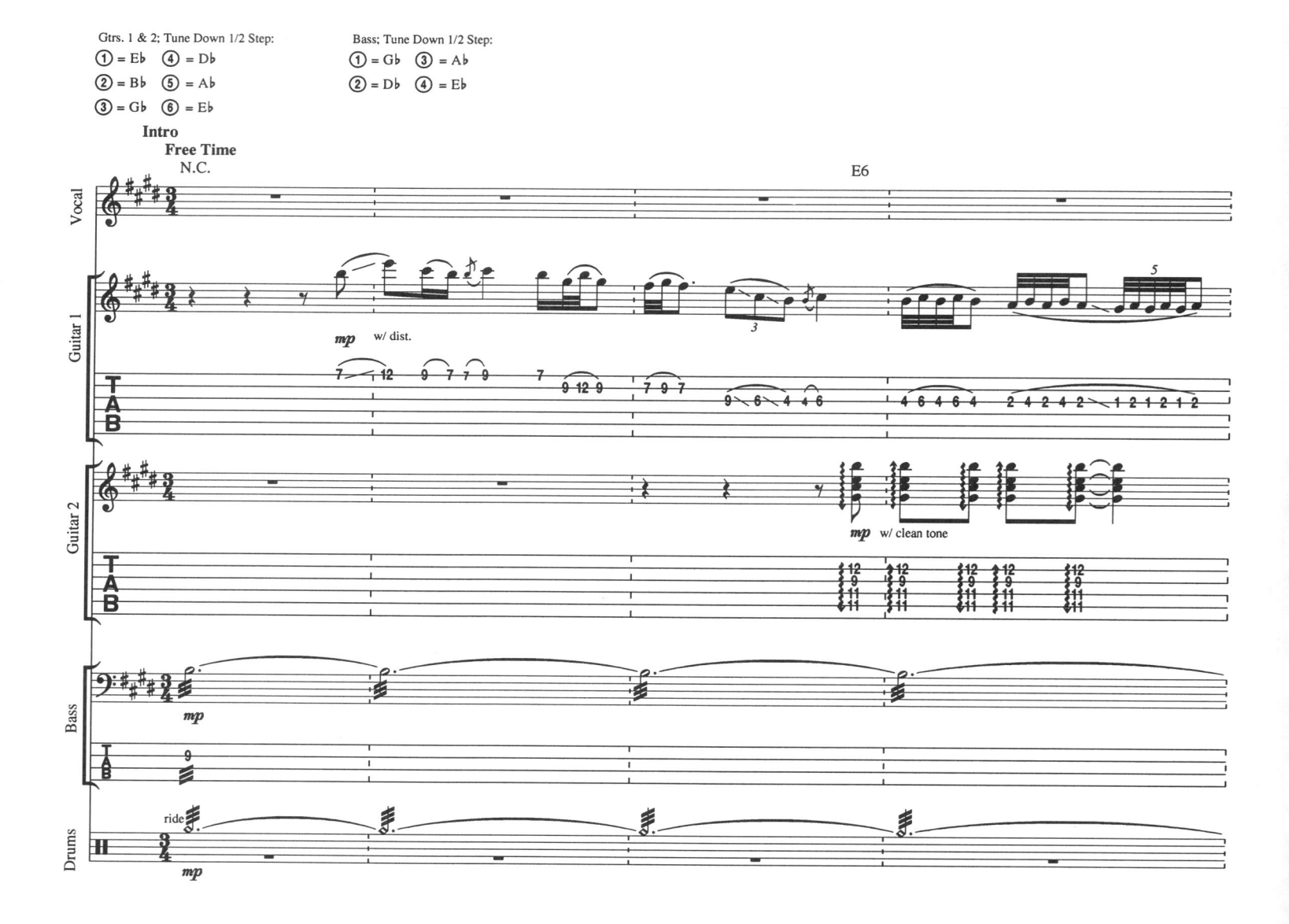

Copyright © 1968, 1977 by EXPERIENCE HENDRIX, L.L.C.
Copyright Renewed 1996
All Rights Controlled and Administered by EXPERIENCE HENDRIX, L.L.C.
All Rights Reserved

141

Vocal
Guitar 1
Guitar 2
Bass
Drums
C#m
E
A
E
go. A mist-y blue and the li-lac too, _ a nev-er to grow
1/2
C#m
E
A
old. ___ A there you were un-der the tree of song,
*T
T T
*T = Thumb on ⑥

Lyrics: sleep-ing so peace-ful-ly. In your hand a flow-er played, a wait-ing there for me.

*Double tracked vocal.

Lyrics:
*I have never laid eyes on you, a like before this timeless day. Ah, but you walked and ya once

smiled my name __ and you stole __ my heart __ a-way, __ ah, stole my heart a-

Guitar Solo

way, lit-tle girl, yeah. __ Al-right!

146

not too long a go. Mist-y blue and li- lac too, a nev- er to grow old.

Vocal
Guitar 1
Guitar 2
Bass
Drums
E
A
A gold - en __ rose, the col - or of the dream I had.
8va
let ring
full
E
C#m
E
D5
Mist - y blue and li - lac too. __
Gold - en __ rose, the col - or of the

A
E
C#m
Vocal
dream I had.
Mist - y blue and
li - lac too.
Guitar 1
8va
loco
Guitar 2
let ring
Bass
Drums
Gold - en rose,
gold - en rose,
gold - en rose.

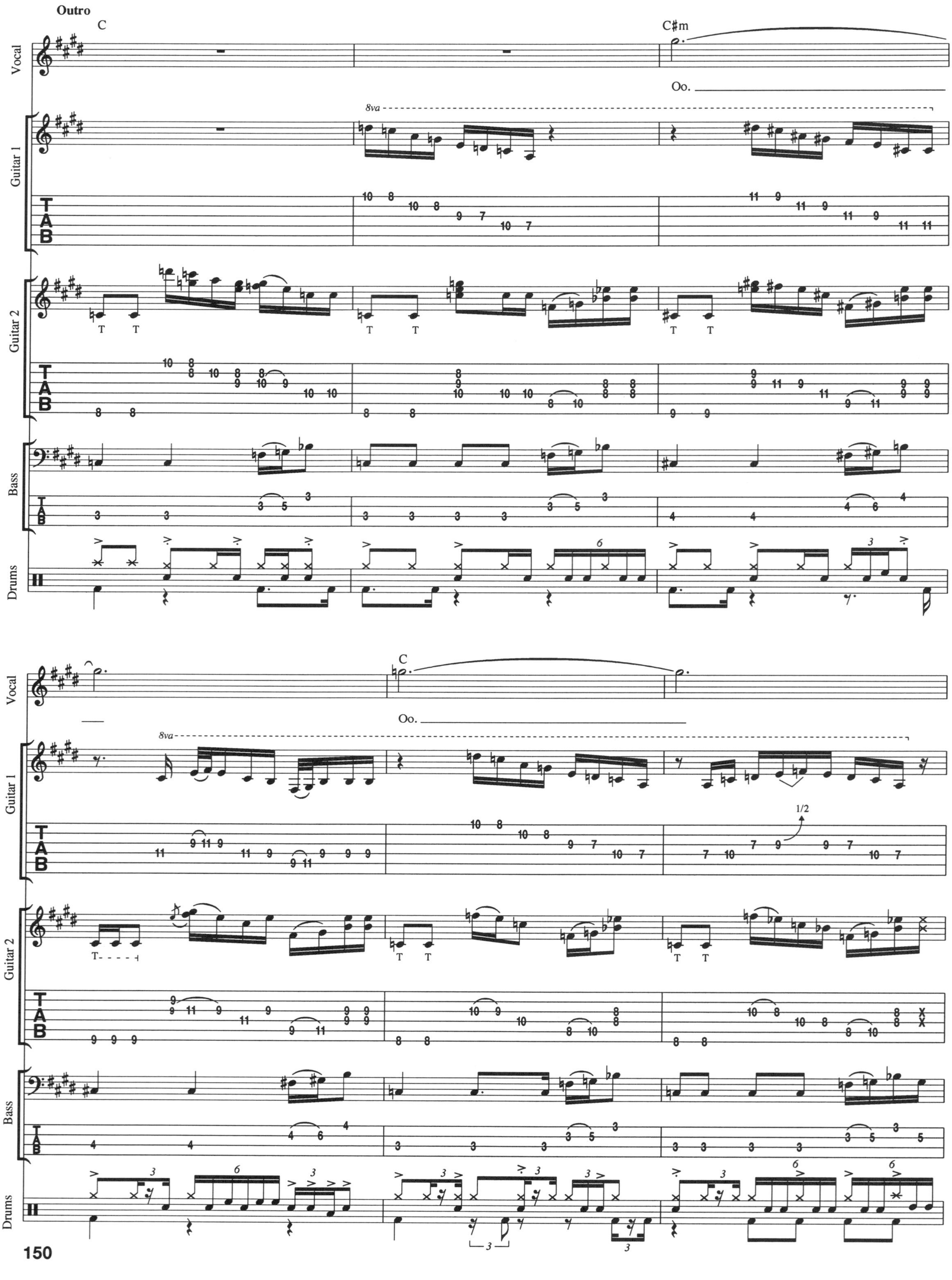
Outro
C
C♯m
Vocal
Oo.
Guitar 1
8va
Guitar 2
Bass
Drums
C
Oo.
1/2

C♯m
Vocal
Oo.
Guitar 1
8va
Guitar 2
Bass
Drums
C
Vocal
Oo.
Guitar 1
loco
Guitar 2
Bass
Drums

Spoken: It's only a dream. I'd love to tell somebody about this dream. The

sky was filled with a thou-sand stars, _____ while the sun kissed the moun-tains blue. And elev - en moons _____ played _ a-cross the rain - bows

Begin Fade

a - bove me and you. Gold - en rose, _

154

the col-or of the vel-vet walls, sur-rounds us.

Little Miss Lover

Words and Music by Jimi Hendrix

Mitch Mitchell's intro figure to "Little Miss Lover" exemplifies his uncanny knack for creating drum parts based on Hendrix's riffs. Other examples can be found in the introductions to "I Don't Live Today" and "Voodoo Chile (Slight Return)."

Throughout the verses, Jimi's guitar assumes the character of a percussion instrument, the result of using a wah-wah pedal in conjunction with muted strings. Going into the lead break he switches on his Octavia, playing a solo that practically covers the gamut of bends idiomatic to the rock and blues genre. Just in case you're a novice to string-bending, take heed and be sure to place all available digits behind the finger executing the bend for additional leverage and support. Most bends are done with the ring finger of the fretting hand, so your index and middle fingers will be the ones assisting in pushing a string up to the required pitch.

Gtrs. 1 & 2; Tune Down 1/2 Step:
① = Eb   ④ = Db
② = Bb   ⑤ = Ab
③ = Gb   ⑥ = Eb

Bass; Tune Down 1/2 Step:
① = Gb   ③ = Ab
② = Db   ④ = Eb

Intro

Moderate Rock ♩ = 98

* Doubled octaves throughout song may be the result of doubletracking, the use of an 8-string bass, or an early-model octave pedal.

Copyright © 1968, 1977, 1980 by EXPERIENCE HENDRIX, L.L.C.
Copyright Renewed 1996
All Rights Controlled and Administered by EXPERIENCE HENDRIX, L.L.C.
All Rights Reserved

Verse
F#9
F#7#9
Vocal
1. Lit-tle Miss Lov - er, heh, a-where
Guitar 1
w/ wah-wah & dist.
Bass
Drums
sizzle cym.
F#7
F#7#9
F#7
F#7#9
A7
A7#9
have you been in this world for so long?
Well, I love a lov - er,

A7
A7♯9
F♯7
F♯7♯9
F♯7
F♯7♯9
Vocal
ah, that-a feels like you. Would ya like to tag a-long?
Well, I
Guitar 1
Bass
Drums
C♯m7
E9
F9
F♯7
F♯7♯9
F♯7
F♯7♯9
real-ly don't need an-y help lit-tle girl, but I think you can help me out an-y-way.
Spoken: Aw, ss-sock it to me.
2. Uh,
hi-hat
ride
hi-hat
ride

Verse
F#7 F#7#9 F#7 F#7#9 F#7 F#7#9 F#7 F#7#9
would you be-lieve baby, I've been look-in' for a soul that feels like you for some
Vocal
Guitar 1
TAB
Bass
hi-hat
ride
Drums
F#7 F#7#9 A7 A7#9 A7 N.C.
time? Ex - cuse me while I see if the
rake
full

gyp-sy in me is right, if you don't mind. Well, he sig-nals me o - kay, so I think it's safe to say I'm gon-na make a play. *Spoken:* Aw, yeah, ha, - ha.

Interlude

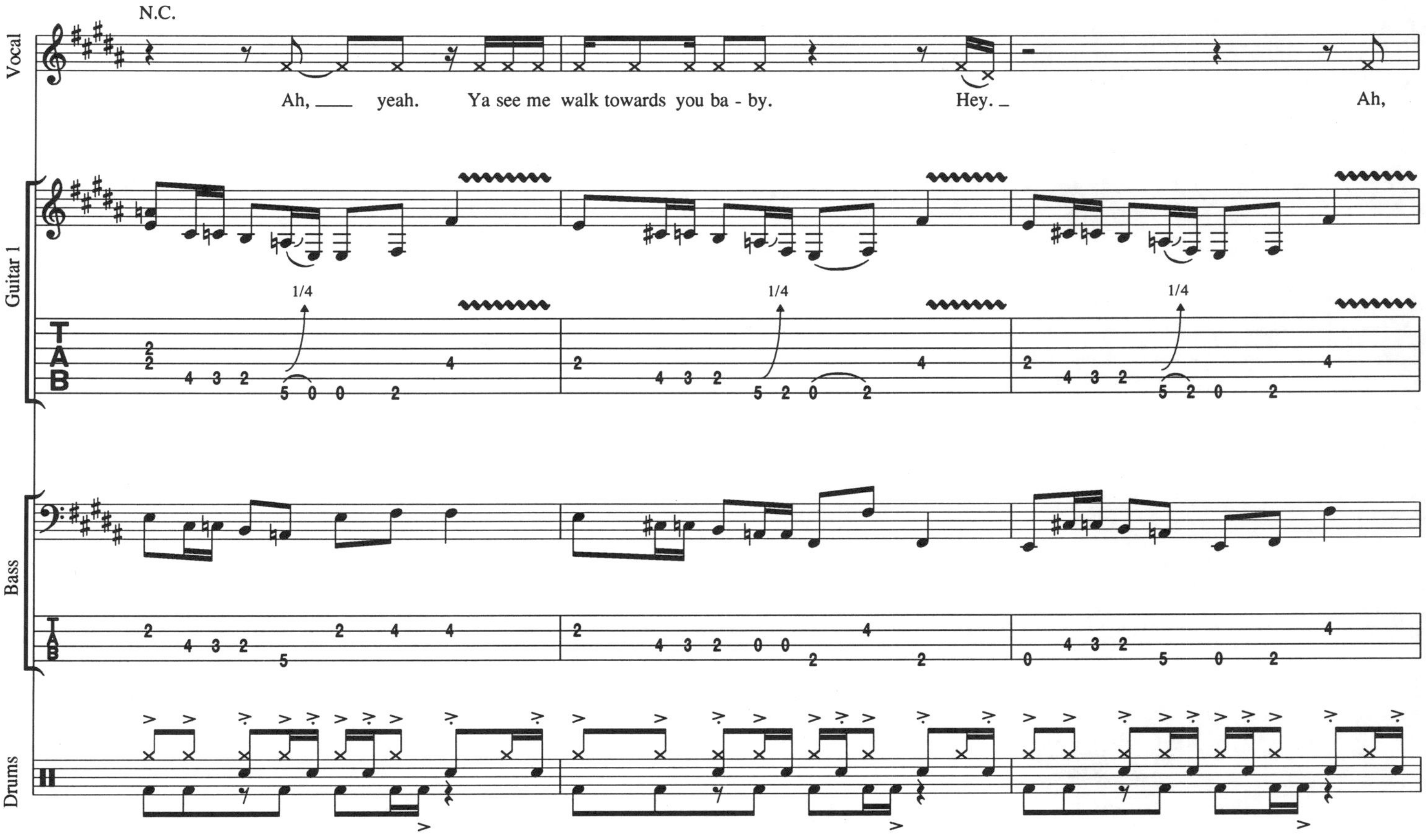

Guitar Solo

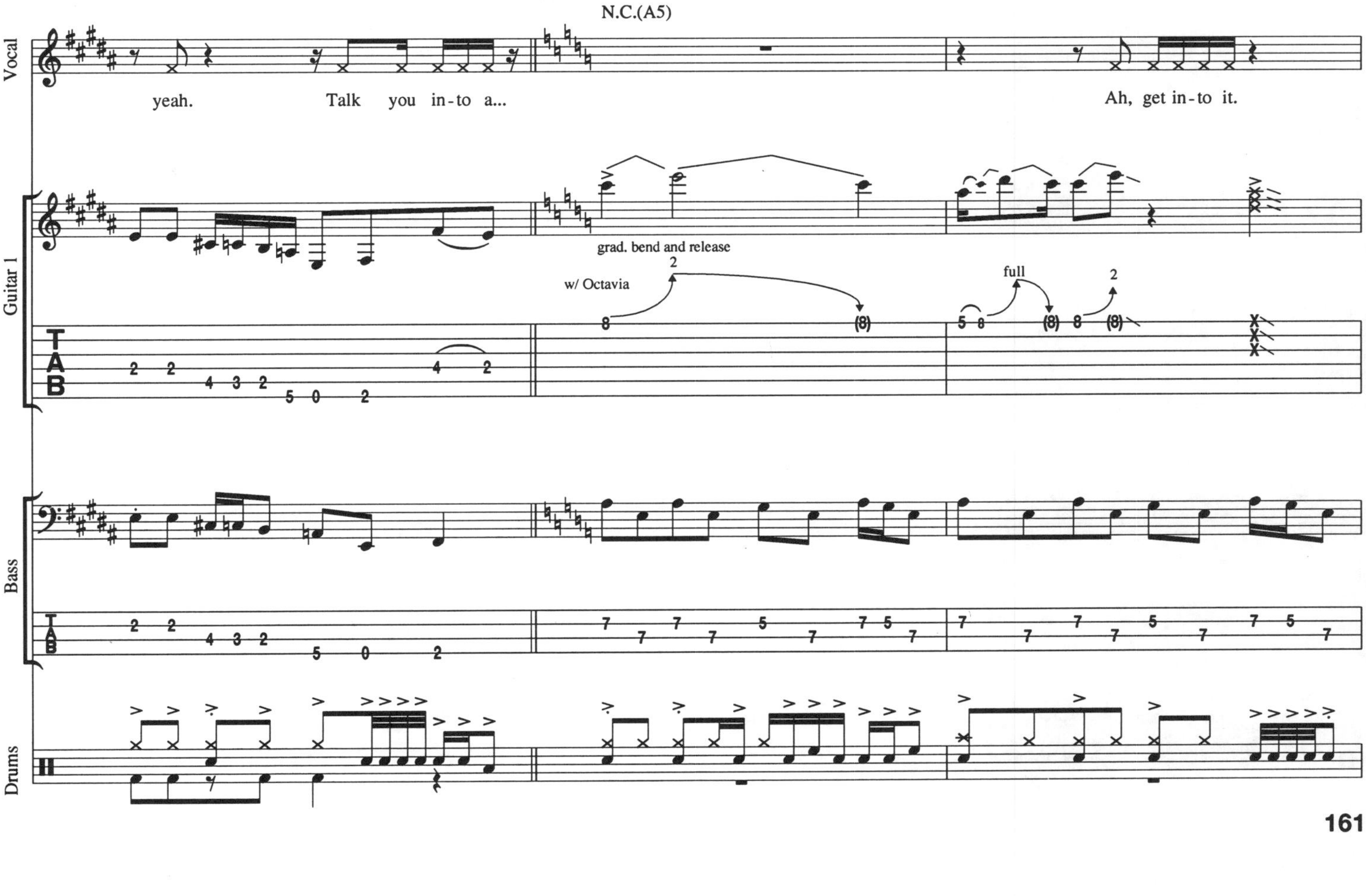

162

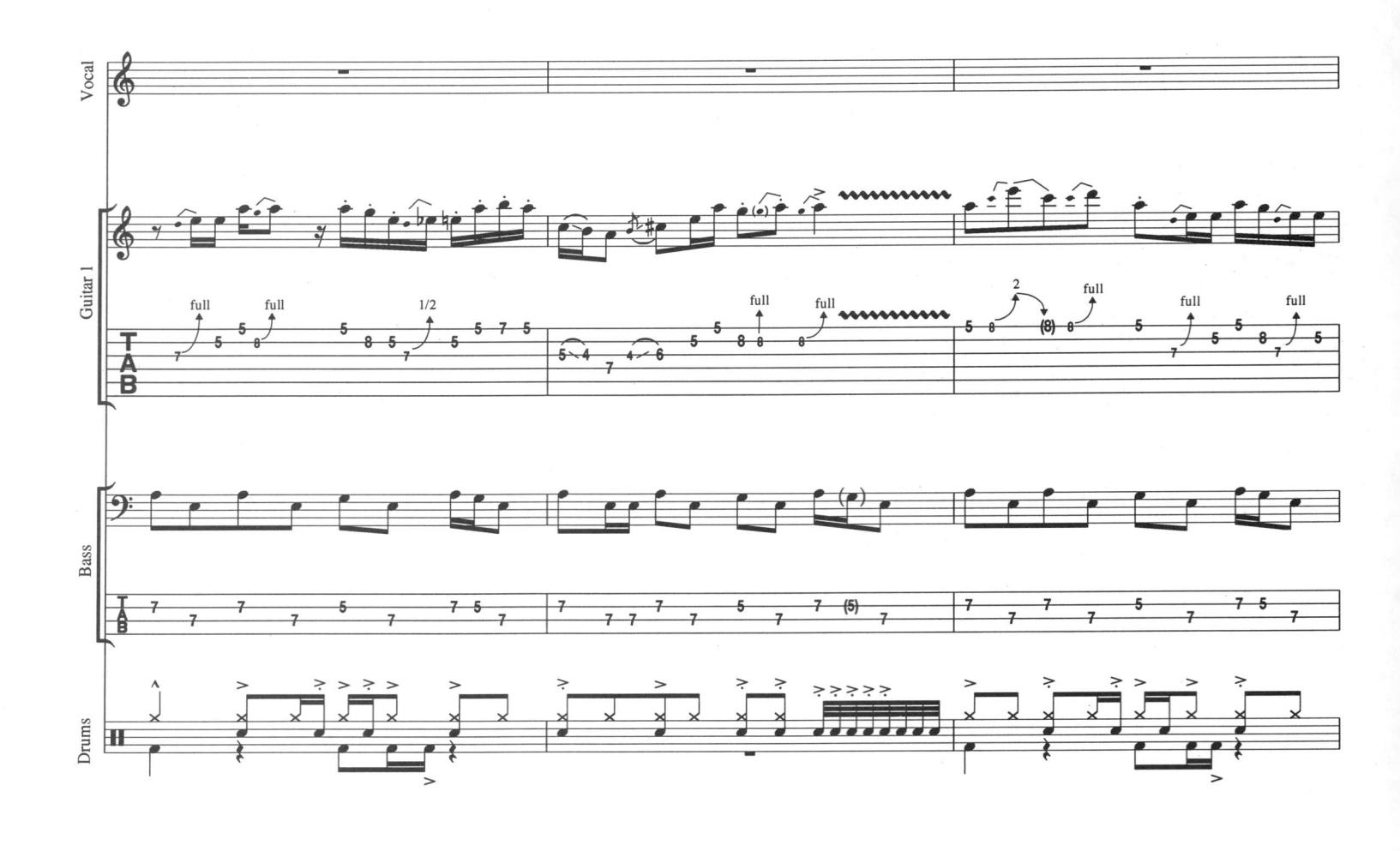

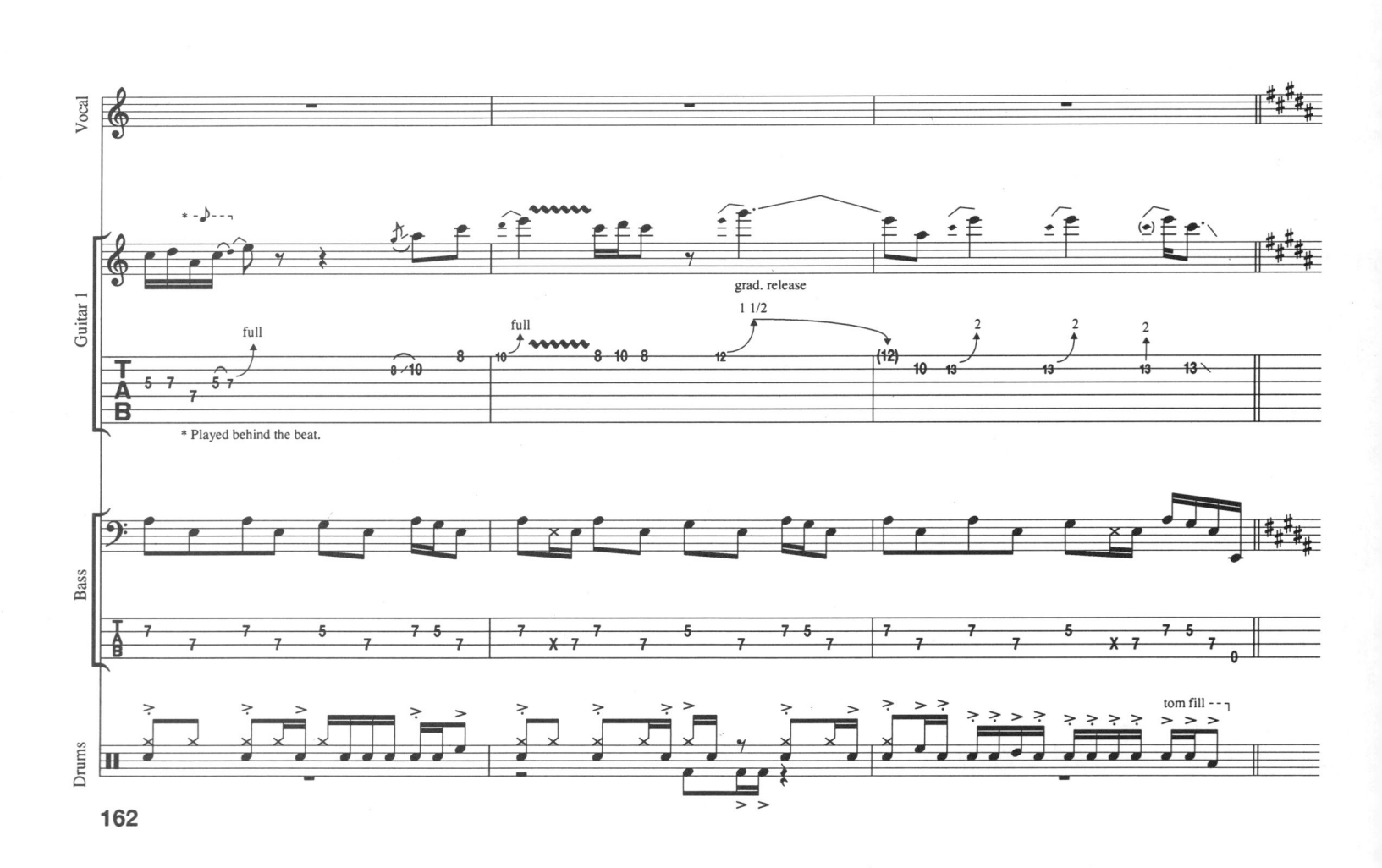

Chorus
F#7#9
Vocal
Hey, hey, lit-tle Miss Lov - er, well, now there's so much you and me can dis -
Voc. Fig. 1
Hey, lit-tle Miss
Guitar 1
* Vib. top note only
P.M.
Bass
hi-hat
ride
Drums
w/ Voc. Fig. 1, 2 times
F#9
F#7#9
cov - er. Spoken: But I think we should start, ah, yeh, think we should start right now, ba-by. Hey,
End Voc. Fig. 1
Lov - er.
1/4

164

165

Bold As Love

Words and Music by Jimi Hendrix

The flower of Jimi's lyrical genius is in full bloom throughout *Axis: Bold As Love*, especially the title cut, with its imagery and personification of the colors. "Lyrical" is also an apt adjective for his guitar playing, whether it be the chordal counterpoint within the verses or the lead lines during the majestic outro solo.

Examining the guitar solo from a theoretical standpoint will reveal why it works in relationship to the chord progression and should help you in developing your own melodies. For example, the solo commences on the root of the A major chord in the form of a string bend, then it moves along to roots of the next two chords in the progression, E major and F# minor. In the third and fifth measures he bends to C#, which is the third of the A major triad (A C# E), then releases it back to B, the fifth of the E major triad (E G# B).

Following this section, Mitch plays a brief solo interlude wherein his drums are colored by ace engineer Eddie Kramer with a bit of studio magic known as flanging. Current state-of-the-art technology makes this effect available electronically, but when *Axis: Bold As Love* was produced it was done mechanically. This required manipulating the reel flange (projecting rim) to one of two tape decks running simultaneously, with the thumb and mixing the resulting signal.

The music of the majestic grand finale seems to take flight and "kiss the sky" on its new course of C# major. Note that beginning with measure 11, Jimi uses arpeggios based on the C# - G# - A#m - B - B# progression, and fades out with tremolo picked partial chords.

Copyright © 1968, 1977, 1980 by EXPERIENCE HENDRIX, L.L.C.
Copyright Renewed 1996
All Rights Controlled and Administered by EXPERIENCE HENDRIX, L.L.C.
All Rights Reserved

Jeal-ous-y, en-vy waits be-hind him, her fire-y green gown sneers at the grass-y ground.

Blue are the life giv-ing wa - ters tak-ing for grant-ed, they qui-et-ly un-der-stand.

Once hap-py tur-quoise arm-ies lay op-po-site, read-y, but won-der why the fight is on.

Chorus

But they're all ___ bold ___ as love. ___

N.C.(A)
E
F♯m
N.C.(G)
Vocal
Yeah, they're all bold as love, yeah!
Guitar 1
let ring
Guitar 2
Guitar 3
let ring
Bass
Drums
ride
hi-hat (open)

They're all ____ bold as love. ____ Just ask the

(A)
(Bm)
(D)
(G)
(G♯)
Vocal
Ax - is.
2. My
Guitar 1
mf
Guitar 2
Guitar 3
Bass
Drums
mf

Verse

Red is so confident, he flashes trophies of war ___ and ribbons of euphoria.

Lyrics: Orange is young, full of daring, but very unsteady for the first go round.

My Yel-low in this case is not so mel-low. In fact, I'm try'n' to say it's fright-ened like me.

And all of these e-mo-tions of mine keeps hold-ing me from, uh, giv-ing my life to a rain-bow like you. But I'm, uh,

Chorus
Gtr. 2 tacet
A
N.C.(E)
F#m
G
Vocal
yeah, I'm bold _ as love, ___ yeah, yeah. ___
Guitar 1
let ring
Guitar 3
let ring
Bass
Drums
ride
A
N.C.(E)
F#m
N.C.(G)
Well, I'm ___ bold, ___ bold ___ as love, ___ hear me talk - in', girl. ___

(A)
(E)
F#m
N.C.(D)
I'm bold as love, uh! Just ask
let ring
P.M.
choke on 2
(A)
(Bm)
D
G
G#
the Ax - is.
Spoken: He knows ev - 'ry - thing...
Yeah! Yeah!
full
Vocal
Guitar 1
Guitar 3
Bass
Drums

Guitar Solo
A
E
F♯m
N.C.(G)
Vocal
Yeah!
Guitar 3
f w/ Fuzz Face dist. pedal
full
grad. release
Guitar 1
let ring
Bass
ride
tom fill
Drums
Gadd9
semi-harm.
1/2

N.C.(F♯m)
G
A
E
Vocal
Guitar 3
full
Guitar 1
let ring
T
Bass
Drums
F♯m
G6
N.C.(A)
(E7)
(F♯m)
(G)
semi-harm.
tom fill

(A)
(E7)
(F♯m)
(G)
(G♯)
Vocal
Guitar 3
Guitar 1
Bass
Drums
full
1/2
semi-
harm.
1 1/2
Slower ♩ = 66
D5
A5
full 1/2
mp

A5
D5
A5
Vocal
Guitar 3
Guitar 1
Bass
Drums
full
1/2
poco rit.
1/2
tom fill
* w/ heavy flange
N.C.
A Tempo
tom fill
tom fill
tom fill
rit.

Outro Solo

*Chords played to Mellotron (early kybd. sampler that utilized tapes vs. electronics) for remainder of tune.

*2nd string sounds unintentionally.

C♯
G♯
A♯m
B
B♯
Guitar 3
Bass
Drums
1 1/2
1/2
full
* fdbk.
* Microphonic fdbk. not caused by string vibration.
tom fill
* Played ahead of the beat.

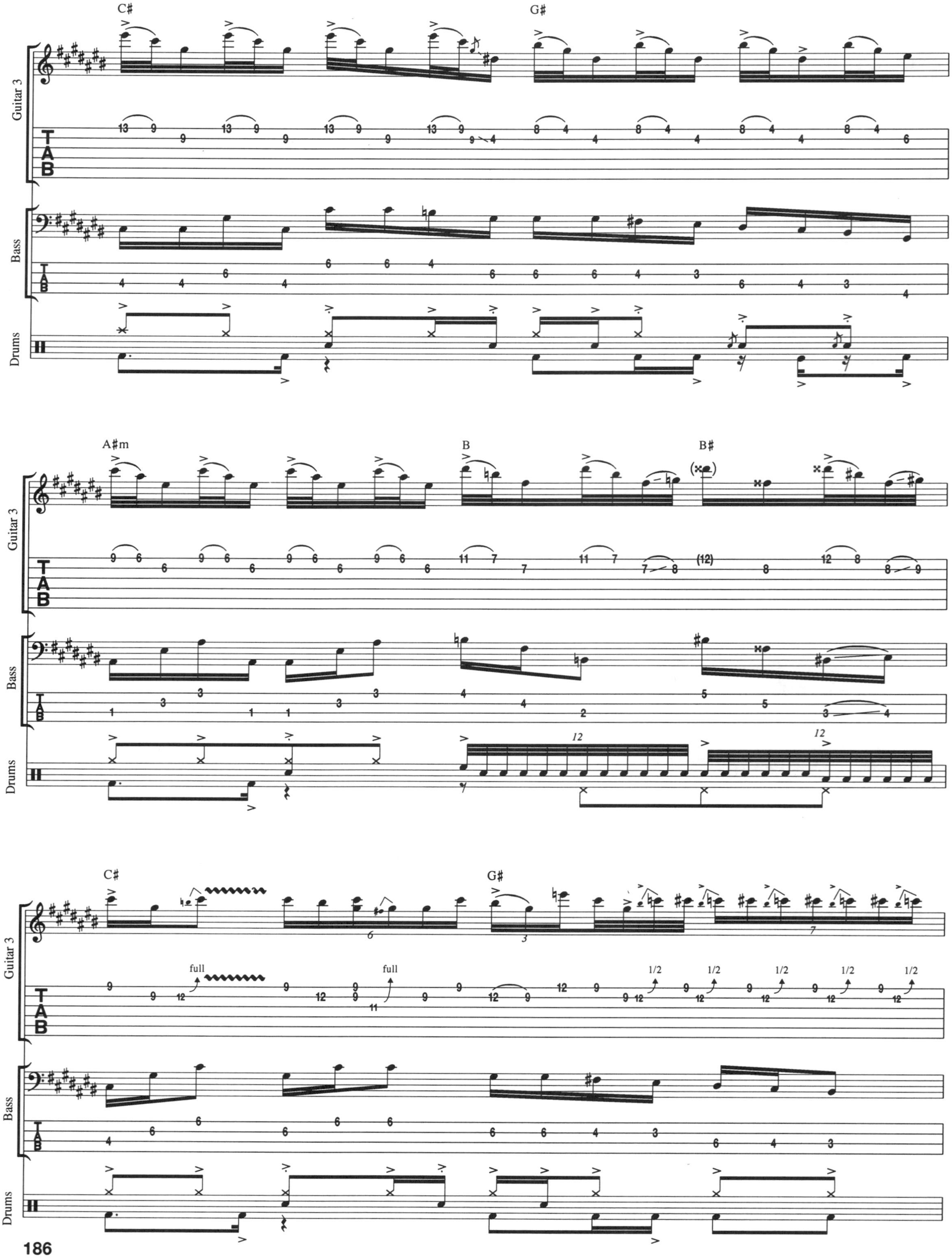
C♯
G♯
Guitar 3
Bass
Drums
A♯m
B
B♯
12
C♯
G♯
full
1/2

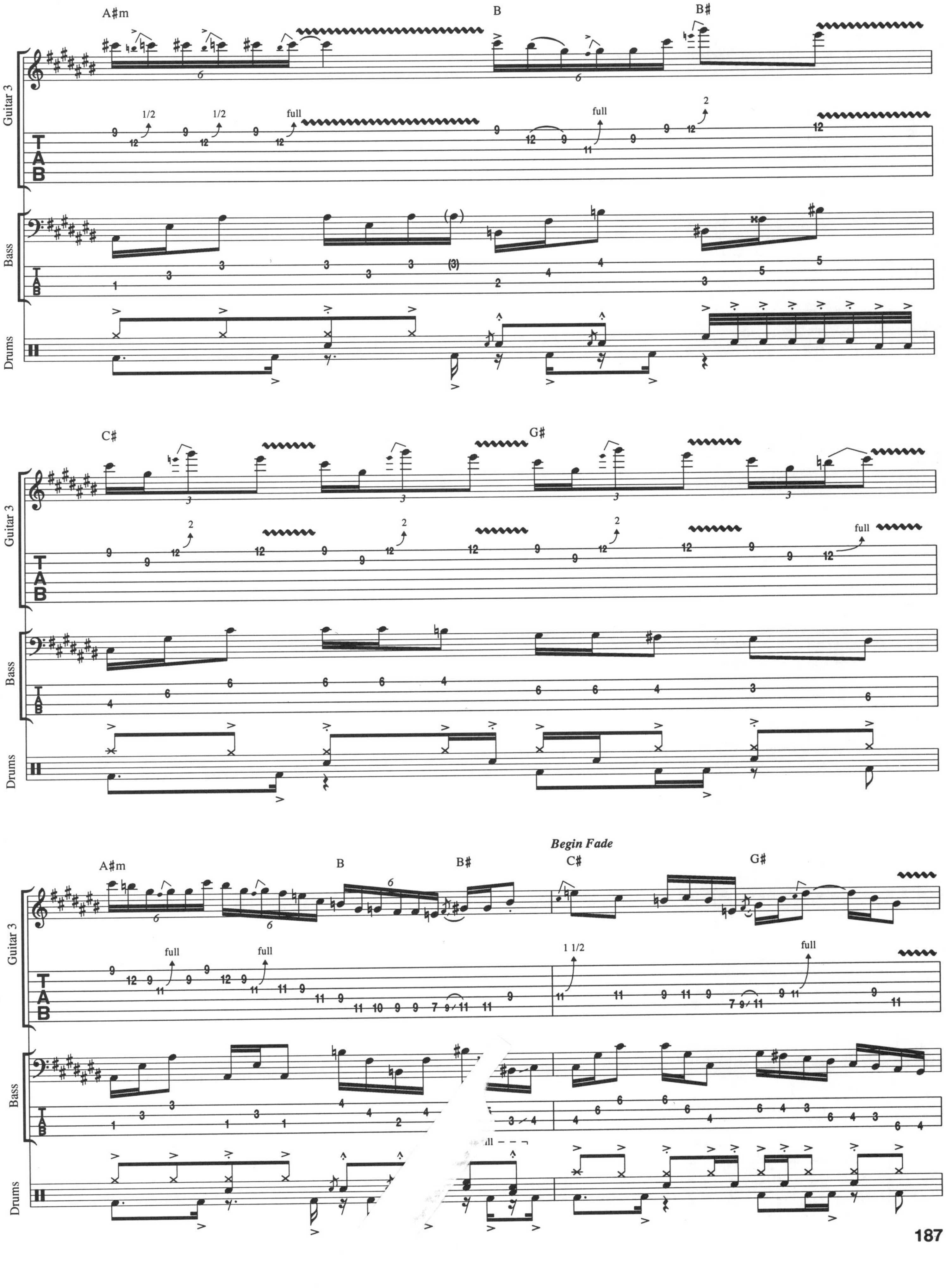
A♯m
B
B♯
C♯
G♯
Begin Fade
Guitar 3
Bass
Drums
1/2
full
2
1 1/2

A#m
B
B#
C#
G#
Guitar 3
full
Bass
Drums
Fade Out
* Trem. pick and slide up simultaneously.

NOTATION LEGEND

BASS NOTATION LEGEND

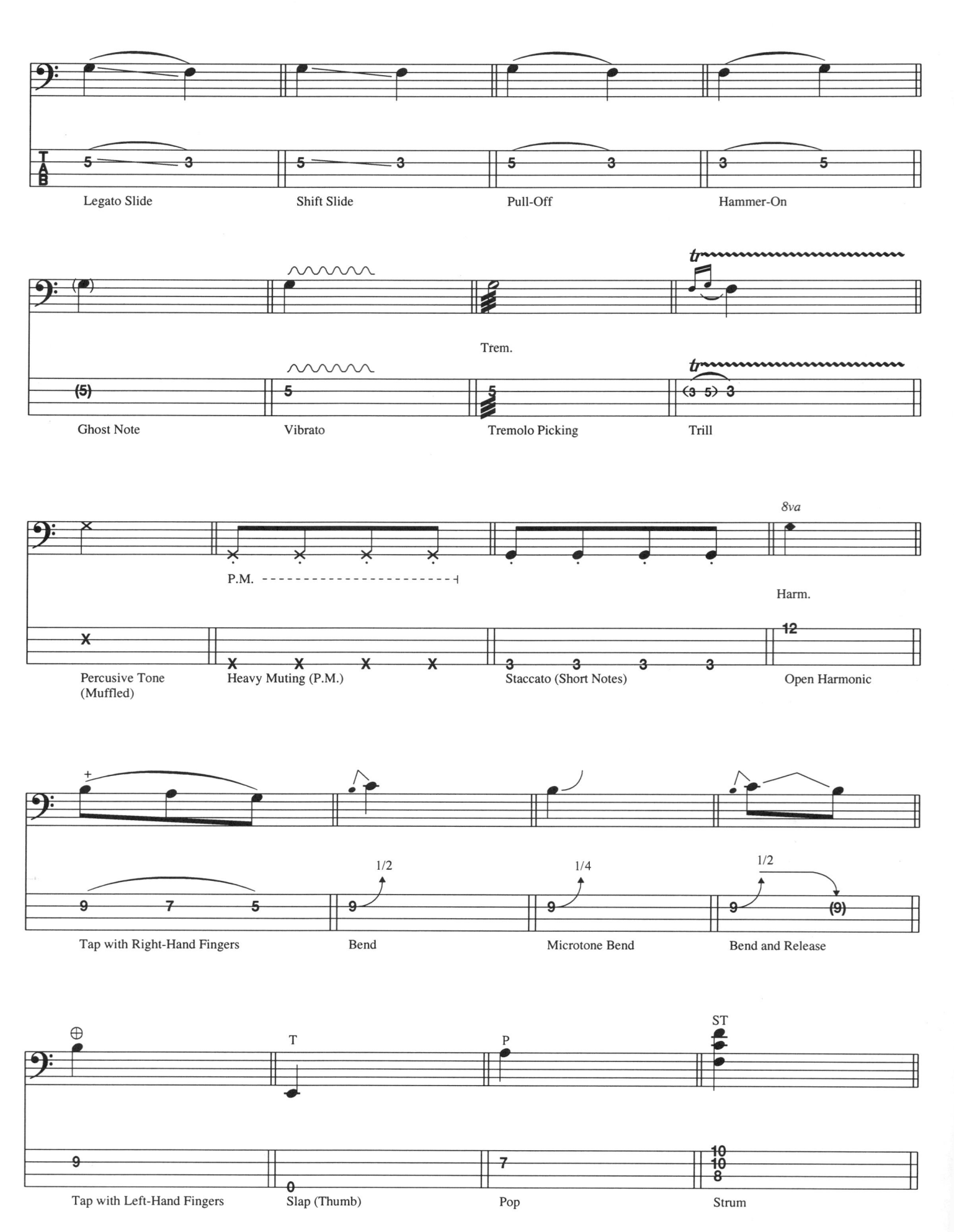

Study the master with these transcriptions and explorations of the techniques and tunes that made Hendrix a legend.

Guitar Recorded Versions folios feature complete transcriptions for guitar plus rare photos and extensive introductions. Easy Recorded Versions feature guitar transcriptions with the harder solos removed. Transcribed Scores feature note-for-note transcriptions in score format for *all* the instruments in each recording. All books include notes and tablature.

Are You Experienced
11 songs from the album including: Are You Experienced • Foxey Lady • Hey Joe • Manic Depression • Purple Haze • The Wind Cries Mary • and more.

00692930 Guitar Recorded Versions $19.95
00660097 Easy Recorded Versions $12.95
00672308 Transcribed Scores (17 songs) $29.95

Axis: Bold As Love
13 songs from the album, including: Bold As Love • Castles Made of Sand • Little Wing • Spanish Castle Magic • and more.

00692931 Guitar Recorded Versions $22.95
00660195 Easy Recorded Versions (12 songs) $12.95
00672345 Transcribed Scores $29.95

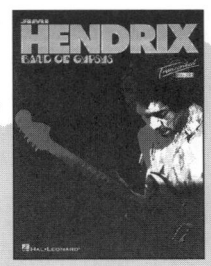

Band of Gypsys
Contains note-for-note transcriptions of: Who Knows • Machine Gun • Changes • Power to Love • Message of Love • We Gotta Live Together. Includes introduction and playing tips.

00690304 Guitar Recorded Versions $19.95
00672313 Transcribed Scores $29.95

Electric Ladyland
16 songs from the album, including: All Along the Watchtower • Have You Ever Been (To Electric Ladyland) • Voodoo Child (Slight Return) • and more.

00692932 Guitar Recorded Versions $24.95
00672311 Transcribed Scores $29.95

First Rays of the New Rising Sun
Matching folio to the new release featuring 17 songs whose creation spans from March 1968 through to Jimi's final sessions in August 1970. Includes 24 pages of color photos and extensive notes on each song.
00690218 Guitar Recorded Versions $24.95

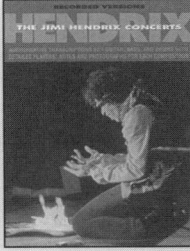

The Jimi Hendrix Concerts
A matching folio to all 12 songs on the live album with authoritative transcriptions for guitar, bass, and drums with detailed players' notes and photographs for each composition. Songs include: Fire • Red House • Are You Experienced? • Little Wing • Hey Joe • Foxy Lady • Wild Thing • and more.
00660192 Guitar Recorded Versions $24.95

Radio One
A matching folio to all 17 songs on the album of Jimi's live radio studio performance. Includes authoritative transcriptions for guitar, bass and drums with detailed players' notes and photographs for each composition. Songs include: Hear My Train a Comin' • Hound Dog • Fire • Purple Haze • Hey Joe • Foxy Lady • and more.
00660099 Guitar Recorded Versions $24.95

Woodstock
Relive Hendrix's Woodstock performance with these 11 guitar transcriptions plus an introduction and photos. Songs include: Red House • The Star Spangled Banner • Villanova Junction • and more.

00690017 Guitar Recorded Versions $24.95

South Saturn Delta
Matching folio to the recent release of 15 tracks, including lost gems like "Tax Free," "Look Over Yonder," and "Pali Gap," as well as previously unreleased recordings like "Here He Comes (Lover Man)," "Message to the Universe" and "Midnight Lightning," and more.
00690280 Guitar Recorded Versions $24.95

Experience Hendrix – Book One Beginning Guitar Method
by Michael Johnson
This book/CD pack has been designed to guide you through a step-by-step process of learning music and guitar basics using the songs of Jimi Hendrix! It teaches guitar basics, music basics, music/guitar theory, scales, chords, transposing and progressions, basics of songs, blues, reading music and includes guidelines for practicing, tips on caring for your guitar, and much more. The accompanying CD includes actual Hendrix tracks to practice with, and on-line support for the method is provided by the Experience Hendrix website.
00695159 Book/CD Pack $14.95

FOR MORE INFORMATION, SEE YOUR LOCAL MUSIC DEALER, OR WRITE TO:

HAL•LEONARD® CORPORATION
7777 W. BLUEMOUND RD. P.O. BOX 13819 MILWAUKEE, WI 53213

Prices and availability subject to change without notice.